The
Collector's
Handbook

42914

The
Collector's
Handbook

Tax Planning, Strategy and Estate
Advice for Collectors and Their Heirs

James L. Halperin, Gregory J. Rohan
and
Mark J. Prendergast

Edited by
Noah Fleisher, Meredith Meuwly and Steve Roach

IvyPress, Inc.

Dallas, Texas

IvyPress, Inc.

By James L. Halperin, Gregory J. Rohan and Mark J. Prendergast

Edited for 2016 by Mark Prendergast, Noah Fleisher, Meredith Meuwly and Steve Roach.

Copyright© 2000, 2004, 2007, 2008, 2009, 2011, 2012, 2013, 2014, 2015, 2016 by James L. Halperin and Gregory J. Rohan

Ivy Press
3500 Maple Avenue, 17th Floor
Dallas, Texas 75219-3941

This publication is designed to provide accurate and authoritative information with respect to the subject matter covered. It is provided with the understanding that neither the authors nor the publisher are engaged in rendering legal, accounting, or other professional advice. If legal advice or other expert assistance is required, the services of a competent professional should be sought.

Choose the members of your financial team wisely, and don't be afraid to pay for good advice; it will save you money in the long run. You will likely need a CPA, a lawyer, a financial planner, and an insurance agent to execute the planning recommended in this book. Encourage your entire team to work together; a financial plan is only as good as it is holistic. Please remember that tax planning is an ongoing process and not an annual event. Collectors have special needs, and tax laws affect different collectors differently.

ISBN: 978-1-63351-302-0

Manufactured in the United States of America
©2016, Revised Edition

Copyright© Cover Design by Wendie Goers, 2016

A True Collector's Mentality

"My wish is, so that my drawings, my prints, my curiosities, my books, in a word, those things of Art which have been the joy of my life shall not be consigned to the cold tomb of a museum, and subjected to the stupid glance of the careless passer-by; but I require that they shall all be dispersed under the hammer of the auctioneer, so that the pleasure which the acquiring of each one has given to me, shall be given again, in each case, to some inheritor of my own tastes."

From the will of Edmond de Goncourt, 1896

"…helpful summaries about care of collections, security, and tax pitfalls." – The Philadelphia Inquirer

"Minimize inheritance headaches and heartaches… Experts' tips for winning encounters with coin dealers and the IRS." – The Centinel

"To those of us in the business of helping remove obstacles from the financial paths of clients, *The Collector's Handbook* is a valuable resource I would think that any advisor would want to have in their library."
- Jeffrey Turner, Certified Financial Planner™ professional, President of Chattanooga Estate Planning Council

"…your heirs deserve knowledge and truth about your holdings. Your use of this book should help, and—especially for those of you with a valuable collection—a copy for your heirs would not be amiss." – COINage Coin Collector's Yearbook

"…deserves to be in the hands of any collector of coins, serious or frivolous. It gives excellent advice for maintaining records, caring for, safeguarding and for disposing of a numismatic collection. Dealers would do well to recommend it to their customers – after reading it themselves."
– Col. Bill Murray, Noted Columnist

The first edition of this book, titled
The Rare Coin Estate Handbook, received many of the
comments and endorsements listed above, and was also
Winner of the Robert Friedberg Award from the
Professional Numismatists Guild:
Best Numismatic Book of the Year.
Now rewritten for all forms of art, jewelry
and collectibles, the 7th Edition of *The Collector's
Handbook* received the "Extraordinary Merit" award from
the Numismatic Literary Guild in 2013.

Contents

PIERRE-AUGUSTE RENOIR (French,
1841-1919) and RICHARD GUINO
(French, 1890-1973)
*Grande Vénus victorieuse (Large
Venus Victorious),* 1914-15
Original plaster
71 inches high
Sold for: $545,000 | September 2013

Foreword

....

WHY WE COLLECT THINGS

My friend John Jay Pittman did not start out a wealthy man. Slowly and with dedication, he assembled an incredible coin collection. He accomplished this through relentless study and the devotion of a significant portion of his limited income as a middle manager for Eastman Kodak, supplemented by his wife's income as a schoolteacher.

In 1954, he mortgaged the family house to travel to Egypt and bid on coins at the King Farouk Collection auction, and he demanded many more sacrifices of himself and his family over the decades. He passed away in 1996 with no apparent regrets, and his long-suffering family deservingly reaped the rewards of his efforts when the collection was sold at auction for more than $30 million.

But why did he do it?

On our website, HA.com, we auction many different types of collectibles; what started in 1976 as a numismatics business is now the third-largest auction house in the world — with annual sales exceeding $850 million in 2015 in categories ranging from meteorites to Hermès handbags. Most of our 950,000+ registered client/bidders collect in more than one area, which we can determine through online surveys, free catalog subscriptions, and multiple drawings for prizes throughout the year. Our clients seek many different collecting areas, and for many different reasons.

One fervent collector of historical documents refers to his passion as "a genetic defect." The founding father of psychoanalysis Sigmund Freud, a renowned collector in his own right, thought that collecting was really about sex: "The core of paranoia is the detachment of the libido from objects," he wrote in 1908. "A reverse course is taken by the collector who directs his surplus libido into an inanimate object: a love of things." But more likely it's basic human instinct: a survival advantage amplified by eons of natural selection. Those of our ancient ancestors who managed to accumulate scarce objects may have been more likely to survive long enough to bear offspring—and people who owned shiny objects may have had an easier time attracting mates. Even today, wealth correlates with longer life expectancy; and could any form of wealth be more primal than scarce, tangible objects?

While the thrill of the hunt and a passion for objects—whether it's Lithuanian first-day covers or Alberto Vargas paintings—is what motivates and excites collectors, there are, alas, some housekeeping chores that must be attended to in order to assure that you derive the most benefit from your collection. Whether that means minimizing your tax burden, ensuring that your objects are safe from intruders, or maximizing your collection's value for your heirs, a little attention now can save you a massive headache later. It will also help you to get as much as you can out of the top ten reasons Heritage Auctions' clients tell us that they collect (not in order):

1. Knowledge and learning

2. Relaxation and stress reduction

3. Personal pleasure

4. Social interaction with fellow collectors

5. Competitive challenge

6. Public recognition

7. Altruism (leaving a collection to a museum or non-profit organization)

8. The desire to control, possess and bring order to something

9. Nostalgia and/or a connection to history

10. Accumulation and diversification of wealth

Like Pittman, Robert Lesser is a true collector, but also a visionary with the ability to change his own course. He funded his later collections by assembling a fine collection of Disney memorabilia before it was popular, and later sold it for a seven-figure sum after the collecting world had come to appreciate it. Long before anyone else discovered their now-obvious appeal, Lesser assembled preeminent collections of toy robots—museum exhibitions of his collection have attracted sell-out crowds with waiting lines stretching over city blocks—and pulp magazine cover paintings.

Many non-acquisitive pastimes provide similar levels of satisfaction, knowledge and recognition, along with the other benefits of collecting. But unlike home gardeners and tropical fish enthusiasts, serious collectors of rare objects will very often find that they have created substantial wealth—especially if they recognize this as one of the goals of their collections.

Whatever your motivation for collecting, this book will make you a more intelligent collector. Following the advice of our expert team of industry experts, accountants, and lawyers will help you enjoy your collection more and ensure that your heirs can benefit from your legacy.

James L. Halperin
Co-Chairman, Heritage Auctions

William Adolphe Bouguerau (French, 1825-1905)
Fishing For Frogs, 1882
Oil on canvas
54 x 42 inches
Sold for: $1,762,500 | May 2012

Acknowledgements

Writing a book is like forming a great collection: many people will contribute in many different ways. While collecting, we build on the work of dealers, auction firms, friends old and new, and those dedicated authors whose reference books line our shelves. It is no different here. We offer many thanks to the following for their assistance during the preparation of this work:

Wendie Goers, Steve Ivy, Bob Korver, Burnett Marus, Steve Roach, Matthew S. Wilcox, Will Rossman, Richard Freeland, Noah Fleisher, Mark Van Winkle, Meredith Meuwly, and Scott Casey.

William Robinson Leigh (American, 1866-1955)
Land of Navaho (Young Indian Goat Herder), 1948
Oil on canvas
45 x 60 inches
Sold for: $575,000 | November 2014

Whitney Houston's One-Of-A-Kind Marc Bouwer-Designed Wedding Gown Worn During Her Wedding To Entertainer Bobby Brown, July 18, 1992.
Sold for: $15,000 | June 2016

Introduction

Collectors know the joy that comes from being surrounded by wonderful objects. The study of the pieces in our collections adds depth, color, and richness to our lives. We also know that a collection is intensely personal and as such, infrequently shared with others. You know your collection intimately. More than likely, your heirs do not.

Meredith Meuwly, our Director of Appraisal Services, remembers the collector who showed up at an appraisal fair with a meticulously-kept book detailing every object she had in her collection: when she bought it, who she bought it from, what she paid for it, and everything she knew about it.

Such meticulousness is rare; all too often, the chaos left behind by collectors' estates leaves their descendants with a tax burden that could have been avoided, along with endless amounts of paperwork, legal fees, wrangling, and other drama.

The principals at Heritage Auctions have written this book to provide information essential to collectors organizing their collections, advisors working with these collections, and heirs who have inherited collections. Organizations that have received collections as donations will also benefit from this book.

Francis H. C. Crick Nobel Prize
Medal and Nobel Diploma Struck
in 23 carat gold and designed by
Swedish artist Erik Lindberg
Sold for: $2,270,500 | April 2013

PART ONE

:
:
:
:
:
:
:
:

Administering Your Collection

Herb Trimpe and Jack Abel
The Incredible Hulk #180
Final Page 32: The First-Ever
Appearance of Wolverine
Original Art (Marvel, 1974).
Sold for: $657,250 | May 2014

Recordkeeping

Mother: "This is the fertility vase of the Ndebele tribe.
Does that mean anything to you?"
Daughter: "No?"   -From the 2004 movie *Mean Girls*

We once appraised a home with six Federal mahogany chests of drawers. The deceased's estate plan stipulated that a certain heir should receive "the good one." While the collector certainly understood which of the six was "the good one," he was not there to help—and the executor and attorney had no idea what he was talking about.

In another case involving a room full of paintings, the estate plan provided instructions for a certain painting: "the one with the banana." The heirs, executor and attorney all looked to us to determine which painting represented a banana. Alas, it was impossible to find any resemblance in the group because all of the pieces were entirely abstract.

These issues sound like vaudeville skits, but both really happened—and they could have been avoided if the collections had been inventoried and numbered. Even when the terms of the will specify the exact location of an item in an effort to distinguish it from similar ones, it may not be enough. As collectors relocate, downsize, or simply rearrange their homes, the location of an item may change. Assigning a unique ID number does not change and therefore remains the only method of inventorying items that we recommend.

Documenting what you own by writing it down by hand or in a printable listing is the most fundamental part of intelligent collections management. For historians and scholars, original handwritten inventories have proved to be invaluable tools in tasks as varied as accurately restoring a historic building, understanding a major battle, or reconstructing a seminal art collection. The oldest known examples of writing in Europe are lists of commodities found in the storerooms of palaces in Ancient Greece. Modern technology has made the process easier than ever, and all collectors must understand the importance of proper documentation: It will be essential to your relationships with insurers, dealers, auction houses, the IRS, and your heirs. Inputting and documenting each new acquisition as you proceed will make this process manageable.

The first question: handwritten or computer generated? While it's possible to maintain meticulous paper records, our preference is that you use a computer program that is properly backed up in case of computer issues—a simple Excel spreadsheet, a Quicken list, a personal website, handwritten note cards, the MyCollection™ feature on the Heritage website, or even some private software options like Collectify.® While doing anything at all will put you far ahead of most collectors, the more detailed, uniform, and decipherable to the novice eye your inventory method is, the better. Your inventory system must be self-explanatory because you may not be there to explain it. Highly specialized jargon, abbreviations and personal notation codes should be avoided.

HA.com has a free feature called MyCollection™ which allows the collector to keep a private record. For coin and comic collectors, the feature is particularly useful because you will be able to quickly see market values for your pieces. HA.com/MyCollection

---

Different types of collectible property will require different information fields, but a general checklist might run as follows:

- **Object type**: What is it?

- **Title**: Does it have a known or descriptive title?

- **Maker**: Is the creator known?

- **Medium**: What's it made of?

- **Size**: Dimensions and/or weight.

- **Inscriptions**: Is anything written on it?

- **Signature**: Did the maker sign it? Where and how?

- **Subject**: Is there a representation on the item?

- **Date**: When was it made?

- **Manner of Acquisition**: How did you obtain it? Auction, yard sale, etc.

- **Cost/Date of Acquisition**: What did you pay for it? When did you buy it?

- **Location**: Where is the item? A safe deposit box, file cabinet, on loan to local museum? Specifics are important; if it's in a binder, say where. For example, if a painting is in the living room above the sofa, note the location and the date the information was entered.

- **Provenance**: What is the item's history of ownership?

- **Special Notes**: Anything else you would want an heir to know about it? More information is always better. For example, has it been exhibited or published in a catalog?

- **Photographs**: Take a picture of each item in your collection.

- **File Folder**: Keep or scan copies of all relevant documentation: invoices, auction catalog entries, bills of lading, etc.

- **Inventory Number**: See next page.

Auguste Rodin (French, 1840-1917)
Le Baiser, 3ème réduction, designed
in 1886, the reduced version
conceived in 1901, and this cast
executed between 1905 and 1910
Bronze with brown patina.
F. Barbedienne ed.
Sold for: $485,000 | November 2013

The Art of Inventory Control: Tying it all Together

Even the most accurate inventory documentation can end up useless
if it is not "tied" to actual objects. Tying data to an object involves
giving each item a unique inventory number, with which it is tagged or
marked, and then cross-referencing that tag with the written inventory
entry and a photograph.

A useful collection inventory number system should begin with the
year of acquisition, followed by an individual item number; for instance,
2016.001 would be reserved for the first piece you acquired in the year
2016. This is the inventorying system used by museums and with good
reason since it is both predictable and easy to follow.

It is critical that the object, photograph, number tag, and master
inventory do not become separated. String tags and sticker labels

are often used when safe to apply, and they can be removed easily; this is easier with some objects than others, of course. Museums generally look for a part of the object that is out of sight when on display—usually the bottom or back—and put a small strip of varnish down. After it dries, the ID number is written in ink, and when that dries, another coat of varnish is placed over the number. For paintings, one should mark only the back stretchers or frames with the work's unique ID number. Each type of property presents its own numbering challenges. Often, the only solution is to tag the box or plastic sleeve in which an object is stored—but this is not ideal because boxes and sleeves can be switched. Today, bar code technology, microchips and even radioactive isotope staining have enhanced our tagging options. Do your research to see what's out there and what's best for your particular collection. Ask dealers who specialize in the category, and seek out the advice of societies that serve collectors. Find out what the best practices are for each category you collect. A key principal is that a tagging or numbering system should never damage an item.

When photographing an object, write its unique ID number on a piece of paper and place it in the picture field so that the photograph actually shows the object and the number. That way, any loose photograph can be easily identified. Most large collections contain near-identical or duplicate items, which—to the untrained eye—may appear indistinguishable from one another, even though values can vary widely. Many coin collections have been spent by heirs who were unaware that the coins had value to collectors and this fate could be avoided with proper identification.

You will thank yourself in the long run, as will everyone involved!
Finally, maintain a second copy of your complete inventory, with photographs, in a different location from the collection itself. Safe deposit boxes in banks are recommended and it's also a good idea to have an electronic copy stored on a back-up disc and/or online.

When you sell or otherwise remove an item from your collection, make certain that it is noted clearly in your inventory—unless, of course, you despise your heirs and wish to send them on a decades-long hunt for a valuable object you sold 20 years ago.

Detective Comics #27 (DC, 1939)
Sold for: $1,075,500 | February 2010

2

⋮

Caring For Your Collection

"He that thinks he can afford to be negligent is not far
from being poor." - Samuel Johnson

"Never neglect details." - Colin Powell

After being created, all objects age; they act and react over time in accordance with their physical and chemical properties, combined with the environment in which they're stored. Metals mineralize naturally. Paper collectibles are photo-chemically changed when exposed to the light necessary for us to enjoy them. Soft fabrics become brittle and hard substances become pliable. While some changes may take centuries, others take only minutes—and the goal of the collector, like that of the museum conservator or Cher, should be to minimize damage and slow the aging process.

Human contact is the leading culprit of wear and deterioration. Use of an object, whether it is a circulated coin or toy train, takes a toll. For many items, use lessens value, but in others, it raises it. A baseball glove worn out by 10 years of continued use by Ted Williams has greater value because of its history, regardless of the physical condition that results from aging. For baseball cards, part of the value comes from their ability to withstand the long odds of survival: cards cut from recently discovered sheets are seen as second-class citizens. Each category of collectible has its own standard governing the effects of original use on value. Once an object has left its original environment and becomes a cultural collectible, the new owners must endeavor to preserve its condition.

Human touch can harm objects physically and chemically through the acids in the perspiration on our hands. After that, sunlight and moisture are the two greatest destroyers of most collections. Another serious threat is contact with reactive materials, such as a cleansing or sealing agent.

Human Contact

Avoiding direct contact with objects, if possible, is best.

- Coins can be placed in sealed inert capsules, which protect them from both physical and chemical harm. If outside a capsule, a coin should only be grasped by its edge, avoiding contact with its two sides. Paintings should be framed using archival materials, and prints glazed, then framed. Grasp only the frames when examining. Comics should be placed in Mylar sleeves or encapsulated by Certified Guaranty Company (CGC).

- White cotton gloves should be worn when handling anything directly, but be aware that one's grip may be affected by wearing gloves. When examining a valuable ceramic lidded jar, place one hand on the lid and the other under the base, so that the lid does not fall off while being moved. Statues in any medium should never be grasped by their extending parts (for instance, the arms or legs of figural works).

Sunlight and Artificial light

If you have ever noticed a rich dark mahogany table bleached off-white and cracked due to its location near a window or a once vibrant watercolor painting fade dramatically, you have witnessed the powerful effect of light on objects. Prolonged exposure to ultraviolet light may destroy valuable furniture, paintings, photographs, books and textiles.

If you wish to keep your collections in plain view, certain steps should be taken to minimize light damage:

- Purchase windows that filter UV light.
- Place UV filter sleeves over fluorescent lighting.
- Glaze framed items with UV filtering acrylic, not glass (not appropriate for all media).
- Curtains and blinds should be hung to filter sunlight.
- Never locate a light-sensitive object in direct sunlight.
- Keep sensitive works covered with protective cloth; remove only when viewing.

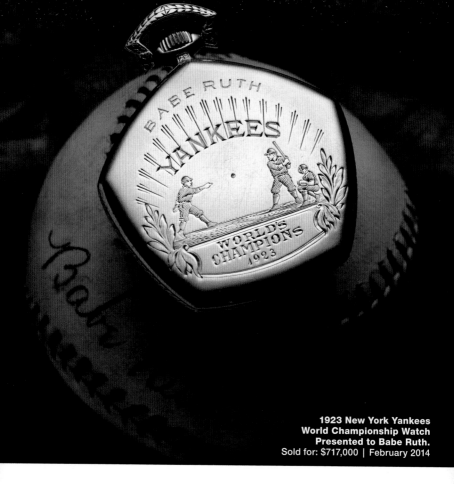

**1923 New York Yankees
World Championship Watch
Presented to Babe Ruth.**
Sold for: $717,000 | February 2014

Water and moisture

> "For my birthday I got a humidifier and a dehumidifier. I put
> them in the same room and let them fight it out." – Steven Wright

Most water damage is caused not by rain, burst pipes or floods, but by
humidity. Organic materials deteriorate in humid conditions; mold and
mildew can grow, and metals mineralize at a greater rate.

The recommended relative humidity (RH) for your collections should
be determined (check with a dealer or society that specializes in your
field) and then take the necessary steps to protect your collection from
air conditioning, humidifying, and dehumidifying. It is important to avoid
large fluctuations in RH and temperature, as these fluctuations may
cause serious stress to any object. Here are the recommended storage
conditions for a few of our most popular categories:

1787 Brasher Dubloon,
EB on Wing MS63 NGC.
Sold for: $4,582,500 | January 2014

- Books: 68 to 72°F, with 40 to 50% relative humidity.

- Comic Books: 50 to 65°F — and it's important to keep
  the temperature consistent. 40 to 60% relative humidity is
  recommended.

- Coins (and other metals): Here, the biggest concern is relative
  humidity. Below 30% is ideal.

- Historic Paper: The Preservation Directorate at The Library
  of Congress says it stores documents at 50°F with relative
  humidity of 50%.

- Paintings: 68°F is recommended, with relatively humidity at
  around 50%.

- Stamps: 65°F and 50% relative humidity is the recommendation
  from *Linn's Stamp News*.

Reactive materials

It is not unusual to find 19th century prints on pulp paper in their original
frames, with acid-rich mats, fixed with glued tape, backed by thin planks
of pine and secured with iron-alloy nails. We have since learned a great

deal about reactive chemistry and understand that the old practices are really, really bad.

The acid in the mat will leech out to the print, causing discoloration or mat burn. Other acids in the adhesive tape will do the same. The wood backer and frame, designed to protect the print, are full of acetic acid, formic acid, formaldehyde and other chemicals that can do serious damage. Finally, the iron nails reacting to the wood and moist air will corrode quickly, harming anything in close proximity.

Today, even our urban, industrialized air contains sulfur dioxide and nitrogen dioxide which can create an acidic environment in the presence of elevated relative humidity.

It is imperative that collectors learn what conditions will affect their particular collections. Outdoor marble statuary will not be harmed greatly by sunlight or termites, but acid rain will quickly do the job unless a protective wax is applied regularly. Some modern art is created with materials that are meant to change over time and that change is part of the artist's intention. Every category of art, antiques and collectibles has its own preservation requirements.

Educate Yourself

Don't assume the frames, wrappers, backboards, plastic sleeves or other materials that house your artworks or collectibles at the time of purchase are the safest ones available for the continued health of your acquisitions. The fact that many collectibles have appreciated in value over time means that a more costly means of preservation may be justified today than when an item was originally sold.

Caring for your collection properly requires learning the safest and most updated methods available for viewing, displaying and storing items. Each object will have unique issues relevant to its own material, form and condition.

Museum and conservation information is readily available in books and online. A good reference is *Conservation Concerns: A Guide for Collectors and Curators*, edited by Konstanze Bachman. For more advice on issues surrounding storage and preservation, check with reputable dealers, auctioneers, and collectors' societies.

Star Power Stallone
·············· The Auction

Most collectors get to a point where they decide to downsize, and this includes celebrities. Celebrity connections have the ability to increase the value of otherwise ordinary items. Sylvester Stallone called Heritage Auctions when he decided to sell items from his personal collection that spanned his long career in Hollywood.

Stallone wanted to be part of the sales process and stayed through several hours of the first day's bidding, interacting with fans and posing for pictures. "The memorabilia I have has been used and been a part of my life for, kind of hard to admit this, well over 40 years," Stallone said. "It's been in my possession and I've fond memories attached to just about every object. There comes a point, though, when I think that I've used these objects enough and have created enough memories that I can let them go."

Heritage's sale, titled "Stallone – The Auction" took place December 18 to 20, 2015, and included dozens of his most iconic costumes, props and personal items. Some of the items included the leather jacket that Stallone wore as a costume in the first Rocky movie in 1976 that doubled its estimate when it Sold for: $149,000. On the jacket, Stallone reminisced, "I remember when I bought this jacket. It was obviously quite a few years before I ever even thought about Rocky, before Rocky was even an idea. This is what I would wear in my everyday life. And when the time came to do the movie, we didn't have a budget where we could afford an original wardrobe so I thought, 'Why don't I just wear the things that I think Rocky would wear, clothes from my real life?' So, I went in my closet, pulled out this jacket. It's one of those unique times where life imitates art, art imitates reality. This jacket was used in several of the films and it really established Rocky as kind of mythical, dark knight character. You knew something special was going to happen with this individual because he just looked different -- and this black leather jacket set the tone for the rest of the series."

A used leather jacket that would be worth perhaps $30 in a secondhand store, described in the auction catalog as a "Small collar, five button front closure, two front pockets, two distinct pleats at shoulders, black faux fur zip-out lining," became worth nearly $150,000 due to its connection to a great actor and a classic film. That Stallone helped Heritage in crafting the lot descriptions, adding priceless first-hand anecdotes which likely encouraged the robust bidding. In total, 13 bidders competed for the lot with the winning bid being placed online at HA Live.

The Stallone sale realized more than $3 million. Beyond sharing his personal history with thousands of fans, Stallone donated a portion of the proceeds to various charities that assist military veterans and wounded servicemen and servicewomen as well as The Motion Picture and TV Country House and Hospital.

A Sylvester Stallone
Personal Black Leather
Jacket from "Rocky."
Sold for: $149,000 | December 2015

Amethyst, Enamel, Gold Necklace,
By Louis Comfort Tiffany, Tiffany & Co.
Sold for: $245,000 | December 2014

Hermès Extraordinary Collection
30cm Diamond, Matte Himalayan
Nilo Crocodile Birkin Bag with
18K White Gold Hardware
Sold for: $185,000 | September 2014

3

Safeguarding Your Collection

"If you didn't have so much stuff, you wouldn't need a house. You could just walk around all the time. A house is just a pile of stuff with a cover on it." - George Carlin

Crimes against property are on the rise, and the reasons that fine art, antiques, and collectibles are great investments are the same reasons they're great targets for thieves. The current arrest and conviction rate is abysmal, and the odds of recovering stolen goods are even lower. Budget constraints have forced law enforcement to deprioritize property crimes and the outlook for a reversal in that trend is not good. So the only solution is to do what you can to protect your collection against criminals—and make sure that it is properly insured in the event that you are the victim of a crime (or natural disaster).

Security vs. Access

Most collectors want their treasures close at hand to study and enjoy—even though that is, of course, a suboptimal loss prevention strategy. To assuage this, write your own personal security plan and include these elements:

• Security
  Your collection is at risk from theft, fire, water damage and other natural disasters. If you are going to have objects of substantial value at your residence, you should consider several proactive measures to protect them:

• Monitored Security System
  A monitored system is at the core of any security plan. This includes both theft and fire alarms that are monitored externally and reported immediately and directly to police and fire departments when triggered. Hardware can be installed for a few hundred to a

few thousand dollars and monitoring involves a monthly expense, currently around $25 to $75. A monitored security system sends most burglars looking for easier game and puts the more daring ones on the clock. Once the system perimeter is breached, the burglar has only the response time to grab what he can and attempt an escape. This might seem like a pain and a substantial investment, but there is help. According to the Insurance Information Institute, the average homeowner's insurance discount provided based on the presence of a monitored security system is between 15 and 20 percent and according to the Electronic Security Association, the average loss on a home with a system is nearly half of that with an unprotected home. But wait! There's more! You'll also be protecting your neighborhood as a whole: A 2009 study out of the School of Criminal Justice at Rutgers University found that the higher the percentage of homes in a neighborhood that have security systems, the fewer break-ins there are in that neighborhood—providing a benefit even to residents who don't have a security system.

- Home Safe
  Safes are obvious deterrents against theft and have additional value in the event of fire or natural disaster. Costs are based on size and fire (temperature) "TL" rating. You should make your determination only after discussing your particular needs with an expert. Many insurance companies require a home safe to write a collectibles rider to your Homeowner's Policy.

- Deterrent Practices
  There are other actions that will reduce the risk of a successful burglary. Always leave the impression that someone is at home. This can be accomplished in part by remembering to have your paper and mail held while you are out of town and by placing one or more of your lights on timers. "Beware of Dog" signs are helpful in warding off potential burglars and can reduce your Halloween expenditures as well.

- Camouflaging valuables
  Most people are predictable, and experienced burglars know all the "good" hiding places. Things you should know to avoid: most

people keep their valuables in the master bedroom and home office. Guess where burglars go first? So, leave decoys. One gentleman we know has numerous coin albums (filled with pocket change) in plain sight on the bookshelves. Another has an old safe that is heavy but moveable. It resides in the corner of his home office and contains absolutely nothing. Its predecessor was removed in a burglary in which the thief left behind several thousand dollars' worth of electronics because he thought the safe was the jackpot. He now has a monitored security system and modern wall safe, but still keeps a decoy as a reminder of the importance of security and the burglar who was the recipient of naught but an empty box (and perhaps a hernia). If you don't own a safe, small valuables are best hidden in a false outlet with an object plugged into it. A collection of small items should be spread over several non-obvious locations.

Off-Site Storage & Transport

The primary off-site storage option is a safe deposit box at either a bank or private vault. If you can find a location close to home or work, the inconvenience factor can be minimized. Sites with weekend access are a major advantage. There is no question that safe deposit boxes offer secure storage, but vigilance is still important. There are still a few storage and security guidelines you need to remember and follow:

• Rent a box that is large enough to hold everything easily.

• Use a desiccant such as silica gel to remove any moisture, and change it regularly.

• Never forget that your greatest security danger is in transporting the collectibles to and from the box. Use a nondescript container to hold them, and try not to carry too much weight at once.

• Have someone drive you to the location, or, if you must drive yourself, park as close to the entrance as possible to minimize your time on the street with the valuables.

• Avoid establishing a pattern in picking up or dropping off your collection.

- Be aware of your surroundings when transporting your collectibles. Check your rearview mirror frequently and if you believe you're being followed, do not drive directly to your destination. Make several detours that do not follow any logical traffic pattern and see if you are able to lose the suspect vehicle. Know where the closest police station is and if you can't lose your stalker, drive directly there. We know this sounds a little made-for-TV movie, but it's important.

- Carry a cell phone with you when transporting valuables. A frightening robbery technique is to rear-end a vehicle and then rob the driver when he or she exits to assess the damage and exchange insurance information. You will have to use your judgment in this situation, but if you are carrying valuables and are rear-ended, you should remain in the car and call 911. Don't hesitate to tell the operator that you are carrying valuables and are concerned about the possibility of robbery. If you really believe that it is a setup, don't stop; call 911 and explain the situation while driving to the police station.

Airports have also become a favorite hub for thieves. There is a steady flow of people, noise, and confusion. The usual method is the snatch and grab; the thief targets someone who appears distracted, grabs the briefcase or bag, and melts into the crowd.

A variation is the use of teams of criminals located where baggage is being unloaded at the curb. A few of the thieves distract the victim while others grab the bags, and then all of them make their escape in a waiting vehicle. Your only protection is constant vigilance. You should always either have a grip or your foot on any case containing valuables.

Some people carry a loud whistle when transporting valuables. If someone attempts to grab a bag and you start blowing the whistle, the thief is put on the defensive. Everyone else in the area is confused or startled by the noise and the thief loses the camouflage of the crowd.

Shipping

First and foremost, do not attach anything to the outside of the package that would hint at its contents. When Ty Inc., the company behind Beanie Babies, realized at the height of that mania that boxes were being lost during shipping in huge quantities, it made a simple change: it removed its logo from the boxes, and shrinkage shrank dramatically. If an address contains identifying words—coins, numismatics, gold, antiques, or anything similar—use initials instead. Additionally, look at the container you're using. We recently received a package from another dealer whose mailing address labels used initials, but the shipping person packed the coins in a "Redbook" box that was clearly marked "Guidebook of U.S. Coins."

Pack the items securely so that they do not rattle. Loose spaces (such as in tubes) should be filled. Pieces of Styrofoam "peanuts" are good for this purpose. Make sure that your shipping box is strong enough for the included weight and bind it with strapping tape. If you are using Registered Mail (the preferred method for most collectors to ship small packages containing valuable items), the Post Office has a requirement that all access seams be sealed with an approved paper tape.

Method of shipment involves a decision that weighs value, risk and cost. USPS First Class or Priority Mail with insurance is the most

Diamond, Platinum Ring
Sold for: $380,000 | December 2014

cost-effective method up for packages up to $500 in value. The rate of loss has dropped considerably over the last decade, making this is a reasonable option for inexpensive items that can be replaced. Above the $500 value, Registered Mail with Postal Insurance is both cost-effective and extremely safe. The one caveat is that the insurance maximum for registered mail is $25,000. The Post Office requires you to indicate if the contents exceed that amount but it will not pay more than $25,000 on a claim. If the value exceeds that amount, you will need to send multiple packages or obtain supplemental private insurance.

FedEx, UPS and other private shippers have become popular in recent years. They offer fast, guaranteed delivery with a high success rate. They also offer some insurance options, but rare coins and certain other collectibles are specifically excluded. You will need to obtain private insurance coverage if you use one of these shippers, or you may request that the other party insure the shipment if they have sufficient coverage available and a shipper account.

Insurance

No matter how many security measures you employ to protect your collection, you will also need to acquire suitable insurance to protect yourself. This can be a complicated area, as insurance companies write policies in a language all their own. As a collector, you need to be especially mindful of homeowner's insurance because you will likely require a policy that is different from a standard one.

As someone seeking protection, you need to understand that contract language will generally favor the insurance company, and you need to know exactly what coverage you are, or are not, receiving. That means asking questions and reading every word of every document in every policy you sign. In the case of coins, you need to be particularly certain of what coverage applies when the coins are at home, in a safe-deposit box or in transit, as well as any additional security requirements for each circumstance. Some things to keep in mind:

- Most homeowner's policies DO NOT insure your coin or jewelry collection beyond $1,000 (combined with all other items defined as a "valuable"). Most insurance companies will offer you a rider for more specific coverage but since it's not their standard business, they are typically not very flexible. You will be required to provide a fixed inventory and it would likely require a major paperwork effort to modify the coverage whenever you buy or sell items from your collection.

- Some insurance companies may require an "appraisal for insurance." If you choose a company that has this requirement, guidance is available later in this book. In this specialized field, the best option often comes from a company that is familiar with the needs of collectors. We have listed several companies in Appendix B.

- In the case of collectibles other than coins, you may want to ask a dealer to recommend a knowledgeable insurance company. Not all insurance companies possess the expertise or coverage options that collectors require. Premiums vary, but price is not the only consideration. Find an agent and a company with a good reputation and expertise in the field of collectibles. You may have to pay a little more, but it will be well worth the price if you ever have to submit a significant claim.

- One final note about security: You need to be careful about discussing your collection (and especially where you keep it) with others. Enjoy your collection, but stay vigilant. A little paranoia could save you hundreds of thousands of dollars.

TIPS FOR HEIRS: This chapter contains advice that may be the most important you will read. Seasoned collectors are generally very security conscious, but those who have come into possession of a collection only recently must immediately understand the risks and responsibilities that come with this unfamiliar asset. Take the collection (if it's small enough) to a safe deposit box immediately. Until you have it safely transferred into a bank vault, do not discuss it with others. With larger objects, you may want to consult with an insurance agent about the best method to safeguard them until they have found their next home.

1919 Belmont Stakes Trophy Silver Tray
Presented to Owner of Sir Barton.
Sold for: $71,700 | July 2015

Very Rare U.S. Model 1875 Colt Gatling
Gun on Original Naval Boarding Carriage
Delivered to U.S. Navy February 24, 1881.
Sold for: $179,250 | June 2013

William Robinson Leigh
(American, 1866-1955)
Indian Rider, 1918
Oil on canvas
20 x 16 inches
Sold for: $394,000 | May 2016

John F. Kennedy
Two White House Oval Office Flags
Sold for: $425,000 | November 2013

PART TWO

Estate Planning For Your Collection

SICILY. Syracuse. Time of Dionysius I (405-367 BC).
AR decadrachm.
Sold for: $394,000 | May 2016

4

All in the Family

Every day, there is a story on some website, magazine, or cable news network that illustrates the importance of having a current estate plan. Jimi Hendrix died in 1970—and his estate was subsequently the subject of 30 years of litigation, a very un-rock and roll epilogue to an incredible career. Picasso was revered as a business genius during his lifetime but when he died in 1973 without a proper will, his many heirs were thrust into chaos. It took six years and a reported $30 million in expenses to divide up his estate. And of current note, musician Prince passed away in 2016 without a will, leaving a sizeable estate hanging in limbo.

One recent survey found that half of Americans with children do not have a current estate plan. Most people try to avoid contemplating their own demise, and many collectors are equally reluctant to consider the sale of their treasures. As Woody Allen once told his physician: "Doctor, I'm not afraid of dying, I just don't want to be there when it happens."

Whether you intend to collect to the end of your life or sell next month, much of the same advice applies. Heritage Auctions has assisted thousands of people in disposing of their collections, and more than 20% were heirs who possessed little knowledge of art and collectibles. Sadly, uninformed heirs—who are grappling with grief and an enormous number of administrative challenges—are easy prey for unscrupulous opportunists. Our goal at Heritage has always been to ensure that the fruits of a collector's pursuits accrue to his or her rightful heirs.

Involve Your Family

Many collectors keep their families in the dark as to the scale and nature of their collecting; there are many reasons for this, but consider taking a longer view. Have you thought about the effect that your sudden death or incapacitation might have on your collection? What would you expect from your heirs? What should be done with your collection? Should it be sold? Distributed among family members? Some combination? What will remain after taxes?

One call from a widow took us to a house where we found a dining room table covered with three-foot tall stacks of boxed world coins. From a distance, it was one of the most impressive collections that we had ever inspected: all matching coin boxes, all neatly labeled with the countries of origin. The widow told us that her husband had been a serious collector for more than three decades, visiting his local coin shop nearly every Saturday. He then came home and meticulously prepared his purchases, spending hour upon happy hour at the table in his little study.

We opened the first box, and couldn't help but notice the neat and orderly presentation: cardboard 2x2 coin holders, neatly stapled, crisp printing of country name, year of issue, Yeoman number, date purchased, and amount paid. We also couldn't help but notice that 90% of the coins had been purchased for less than 50 cents and the balance for less than one dollar each. The collection contained box after box of post-1940 minors: all impeccably presented and all essentially worthless.

We asked Mrs. Smith if she had any idea of the value of the collection. She replied that she knew that rare coins were valuable, and since her late husband had worked so diligently on his collection for so many years, she assumed that the proceeds would enable her to afford a nice retirement in Florida.

We had to carefully explain that we couldn't help her with the sale of the coins. Her husband had enjoyed himself thoroughly for all those years, but he had never told her that he was spending more on holders, staples and boxes than he was on the coins. Her dreams of a luxurious retirement diminished, we advised her to contact two dealers who routinely purchase such coins. Mr. Smith's fault was not in his collecting, but in his failure to inform his wife of the nature of the collection.

We more typically encounter widows and heirs at the other end of the spectrum. When your spouse spends $50,000 or $100,000 on rare coins or other collectibles, you generally have some knowledge of those purchases, but not always—and often the most prodigious collectors are coy with their family about just how much they're investing. This leads to the more enjoyable surprises—those made-for-TV moments where we inform unsuspecting heirs of the vast fortune they've inherited.

Years ago we encountered the younger of two sisters who were dividing their father's estate. Dad had left Germany in the early 1930s—not a great time to immigrate to America, but an excellent time to be leaving Germany. Dad brought to America two collections: antique silver service pieces and his rare coins. The coins were mostly sold to establish his business in Iowa. He prospered despite the hard times, and devoted the next 30 years to rebuilding his collection of German coins.

At the same time, he continued to expand his collection of 17th and 18th century German silverware. We knew every aspect of his collecting history, because he left a meticulous record on index cards. Every coin, every piece of silver was detailed with his cataloging and purchase history. His daughter was in awe of his passion for maintaining such detailed records.

After his death, his daughters decided to split his collections between themselves. They added up the purchase values of each of his collections, which were just about equal. The older sister/executor had acquired some small knowledge of antique silver, and since she wished to keep all of the elegant heirloom tea service for herself, she decided to keep the silver and give her younger sister the coins. She was definitely not interested in splitting. She sold the non-family silver pieces through a regional auction house, and boasted of realizing more than $200,000 from her father's $27,000 investment.

The younger sister came to us with only one box of his coins. Her father's records for that box indicated a cost of less than $2,000, but knowing the years he had collected, we were anticipating at least a few nice coins. However, we were totally unprepared for what came next: pristine coins of the greatest rarity. His $2,000 box was worth more than $150,000, surpassing all our wildest expectations.

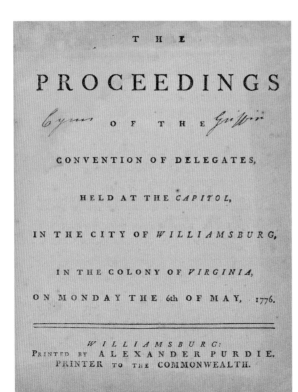

THE

PROCEEDINGS

6 yrs OF THE *Griffin*

CONVENTION OF DELEGATES,

HELD AT THE *CAPITOL*,

IN THE CITY OF *WILLIAMSBURG*,

IN THE COLONY OF *VIRGINIA*,

ON MONDAY THE 6th OF MAY, 1776.

WILLIAMSBURG:
PRINTED BY ALEXANDER PURDIE,
PRINTER TO THE COMMONWEALTH.

Continental Congress President Cyrus Griffin. *The Proceedings of the Convention of Delegates, Held at the Capitol, In the City of Williamsburg, In the Colony of Virginia, on Monday the 6th of May, 1776.* Sold for: $197,000 | April 2014

She then produced the record cards for the rest of the collection, and we offered to travel back to Iowa with her the same day. When we finished auctioning the coins, she had realized more than $1.2 million.

In another situation, the wife of a deceased coin dealer called us to consign $1 million in rare coins from his estate. This asset represented a significant portion of her retirement assets. We eagerly picked up the coins, and had already started cataloging and photographing when we received an urgent phone call from her attorney. The coins had to be returned immediately. It appeared that her husband had been holding the extensive coin purchases of his main customer in his vaults, and he had neither informed his wife nor adequately marked the boxes. Most of her $1 million retirement asset belonged to her husband's client and not to her husband.

A final example that really distressed us demonstrates that partial planning, no matter how well intentioned, cannot always guarantee the desired outcome. A collector with sizeable holdings divided his coins equally (by value) between his adult son and daughter, with instructions that they should seek expert advice before selling. The daughter came to us, and was pleased to learn that her coins were worth in excess of $85,000.

After she signed the Consignment Agreement, she told us the rest of the story. Her brother had "sold" his share eight months earlier to a local pawnbroker for less than $7,500. Her father hadn't shared his knowledge of the asset's value with his children for fear that his son would spend the money foolishly. Instead, her brother basically gave it away.

So, what should you do to prevent such problems?

Get Your Family Involved

If transferring your collection to the next generation is desirable, you will want to provide for an orderly transition. If they aren't interested in sharing your love of the collectibles, you will have to decide whether to dispose of the collection in your lifetime, or leave that decision to your heirs. If the latter, your family should—at a minimum—have a basic understanding of your collection, its approximate value, and how you want it distributed.

Important questions to be discussed:

- Are there heirs who will want the collection from a collector's standpoint?

- Where are the objects kept?

- Where is the inventory of the collectibles kept?

- What is the approximate value of the collection?

- Has the collection been appraised or insured? If, so, where is that appraisal and does it need to be updated?

- Do any of the articles in your possession belong to someone else?

- Are there certain dealers or other experts you trust to provide guidance to your heirs?

• Is there a firm that you and your heirs will wish to use in the collection's disposition after your death?

The horror stories that begin this chapter are all true, none are isolated cases, and they won't be the last. If, for whatever reason, you cannot allow yourself to share this information with your whole family, choose one trusted individual—perhaps the person you are considering to be the executor or trustee of your estate. If that doesn't satisfy you, please take the time to write detailed instructions, or simply make notes in this book, and leave it in your safe deposit box, or wherever you keep your valuables.

The next few chapters will further define your options and help you implement those options. Whatever your choices, the written instructions can be incorporated in your estate plan. At the very least you will have a document kept with your collection's inventory. Your heirs will certainly be grateful for your attention to detail.

TIPS FOR HEIRS: This chapter does not address inheritance issues, but communications can be initiated from any direction. Do you have a parent with a collection? Certainly it is an issue that requires tact, but such a discussion may save considerable difficulty later. Additionally, if you know in advance that your spouse or relative has named you as executor in a will or as trustee of a trust, a few conversations about the collection will make your life much easier.

A Sioux Boy's Pictorial Beaded And Fringed Hide Shirt
c. 1875
Sold for: $75,000 | November 2013

Chris Ivy's Story ....

Chris Ivy is the Director of Sports Auctions for Heritage Auctions. He graduated with a BA in History from the University of Texas at Austin and joined Heritage in 2001 after serving as a professional grader with Sportscard Guaranty Corporation (SGC) in New Jersey.

Heritage Auctions consignment director Peter Calderon was as skeptical of that first call as any reasonable person would have been: a hoard of 700 baseball cards, more than 100 years old and in mint condition, is something that has never happened before. So when a stranger calls you up and says that's what he has, it seems dubious.

But when he showed me the photos on his cell phone, I was intrigued; if it was what it looked like it was, this was a very, very big deal. The next day, the family Fed Ex'ed us a box with eight cards. We confirmed their authenticity and it would have been an amazing find even without the roughly 692 cards that remained, still in Defiance, Ohio, where we flew as quickly as possible because the heirs were concerned about having that kind of value sitting in a home.

The consigner was a man named Karl Kissner who, as the executor of his aunt's estate, represented some 30 heirs who all had a stake in the collection. The cards had been stored in a box in an attic of the modest home for a century, buried under an antique dollhouse. One card had been out of the box during that time, exposed to the elements — and it served as a reminder of what would have happened to the other cards had they not been so well-preserved. But because of that box, we were staring at probably the single greatest find in the history of card collecting: ultra-rare cards depicting icons like Ty Cobb, Connie Mack, Cy Young, and Honus Wagner, all in condition similar to the brand new cards you could buy at WalMart today.

The question of how to sell the cards was challenging. At the time, the universe of collectors for the set likely consisted of a grand total of fewer than 50 people. The 1910 E-98 set was, paradoxically, so rare that few people wanted it. High-end early baseball card collectors tend to be relentless completionists — laser-focused on accumulating whole sets — and the E-98 set was so elusive that few collectors had even ventured to try. The limited universe of collectors combined with the sheer size of the collection meant it would be financial suicide to try to sell the whole collection at once with a mega-auction.

Within the collectibles field it's common for owners of hoards to sell off their treasures piecemeal over time, keeping secret the true size of the collection out of fear that if people know how many there are, they'll wait for the prices to come down — and as a result, the prices will never even start high.

With the family, we decided right away that wasn't the way to do it. First, we didn't think it was ethical — and that if we're to follow the "slow leak" approach, we would end up with a lot of disgruntled buyers who had overpaid for the first few cards only to watch the prices come down. Second, we knew that a cache of this size could attract tremendous media attention — especially if the family was willing to serve as the public face of it — and, with a set with a limited collector base like this one, we thought media attention could expand that market. We talked to the family about how to approach the press and the first question was "What should we call it? What's the name of the region you're from?" They told us it was known as The Black Swamp — and at first we weren't sure about calling it that. It seemed a little dark but we decided that it was intriguing and mysterious enough to attract attention.

So we opted for a sort of hybrid approach: We'd offer the story of the Black Swamp Find to the media, but we'd carefully sell off the collection over the course of four or five years. We put out a press release and the first major story came from The Associated Press. Then local and cable news shows followed and, finally, *Today* called. Matt Lauer loved the story and we ended up having to reschedule the segment because he wanted to make sure we were on when he could do the interview! In all, the story appeared on literally thousands of traditional and online media outlets and will continue to generate press within the trade for years to come.

Thirty members of the family came to the auction for the first few cards from the Black Swamp Find; in total, the first 30 cards we sold realized a combined $566,132. The family understands the importance of patience in realizing full value for the collection, and so it looks like I'll be telling the story of the Black Swamp Find for years to come.

5

Division of Assets

"There is a strange charm in the thoughts of a good legacy, or
the hopes of an estate, which wondrously removes or at least
alleviates the sorrow that men would otherwise feel for
the death of friends." -Miguel De Cervantes

Inheritances bring out the best in some families and the worst in others. The problem is that it's difficult to predict exactly how the prospect of an inheritence will work out in any given family, so it's best to plan everything you possibly can in advance to minimize the potential for wrangling.

In the highly-charged emotional environment surrounding the loss of a loved one, any weaknesses in the relationships of those left behind are exacerbated. Suspicious minds are more finely honed and if the estate remains for the survivors to divide, it won't take much of a spark to ignite a fire. You can minimize the likelihood of a family meltdown by seeking sound legal advice in preparing your estate plan and by leaving precise written instructions for dividing your assets among your heirs. If the collection is of substantial value, you will need to obtain legal advice from experts in tax and estate planning, as well as advisors who are familiar with your particular collectibles. An insurance advisor should always be part of your advisory team, as we will discuss later.

Instructions about collections are particularly important because they generally involve a large number of pieces with valuations that are not obvious based on appearance alone. This can lead to conflict. For instance, in the world of coins and currency, there are a number of varieties and variations of the same coin and date. Without the help of an expert, it is not difficult to make an expensive error.

The simplest option (administratively) is to leave the collection intact, to one heir. The collection should be appraised and, if necessary, submitted to the appropriate grading or authentication service as recommended later in this book, which will establish an equitable basis for dividing the balance of your estate.

The values of items in a collection should not be based on insurance appraisals; when this mistake is made, the heir who receives the collection can came out far behind heirs who receive cash or real estate. Insurance appraisals usually represent a "retail replacement" valuation which can be very different from the "fair market" valuation that would be used for financial planning or estate tax purposes. "Fair market valuations" represent, by definition, a value closer to what a collection might be expected to bring in an orderly sale. Auction houses are a good source for determining a realistic estimate of what an item would sell for in the open market. Most auction houses provide auction estimates free of charge.

If your estate contains more than one collection (and an equal or managed division is part of your plan) you should have the other collections appraised as well to achieve equitable distribution. An attorney with expertise in tax and estate planning can provide the appropriate language. This is considered to be the simplest option, because it stifles any disputes before they arise.

If you divide one collection among multiple heirs, the paperwork burden increases. Our basic advice is don't do this. If you must, you must designate which specific items are to be distributed to which recipients, then expand the scope of the appraisal, and more precisely, define and specify the location of each recipient's inheritance. Alternatively, you may decree "equal shares." This will also require a detailed and comprehensive appraisal, but may cause problems if two heirs want the same exact item(s), or if some heirs want to keep certain articles and others want to sell. You should objectively analyze your family dynamics and the financial situation of each family member in making this decision, along with any special needs that are involved as to those who are unable either mentally or emotionally to act in their own best interests.

We frequently hear the lament that there is no member in the family who enjoys or understands collectibles. We like to think that no one enjoys or understands them yet—but you may not want to count on that in your estate planning. A simpler alternative is to establish an estate plan directing that the articles be sold, with the proceeds shared equally among the heirs rather than enduring the cumbersome process of equitably dividing a collection.

The question then arises as to whether the collection should be disposed of in your lifetime, versus directing your estate to handle the sale. In our experience, it is generally best when the sale is handled during the collector's lifetime. Who would handle the sale as knowledgeably as you would? If this represents a significant asset to your heirs, are they prepared to manage it properly? As properly as you would? Doubtful!

There are also a number of tax issues that must be considered, which will be discussed later. For now, it's important to remember that there are different tax consequences related to gifting assets during your lifetime versus bequeathing them at the time of your death. However, taxes should only be a part of your determination—not the sole consideration. You must weigh many factors in deciding what is best for you and your family.

We understand if you are unable to part with your treasures, particularly if developing your collection is a major activity and source of enjoyment. If this is the situation, we strongly recommend that you prepare a written disposition plan for your heirs and maintain it with your inventory. Whether you intend to collect for three years, seven or a lifetime, you need to prepare now as if you will not be available to provide guidance in the future.

In summary, your collection is yours to enjoy now and yours to sell or give away as you see fit. The old saw says, "You can't take it with you." You can, however, ensure that the collection provides as much value for others as it has for you. We further address financial considerations of selling during your lifetime verses gifting in the next chapter.

Make an action plan for your collection, even if you anticipate many more decades of collecting. You can and should continually revise and update your plan. Postmortem planning is not an option, so speak with your advisors now.

If the timing is immediate, find the advisor or advisors that are essential to the implementation of the plan and proceed accordingly. Otherwise, prepare detailed written instructions and leave copies with both your collection and your estate plan. If you prefer that your collectibles be distributed among family members, provide specific instructions in writing as to how distribution is to be accomplished. If you wish to distribute the proceeds, make certain that you provide directions for non-experts to contact a firm or dealer who is trustworthy, experienced, and reputable. Your instructions should be as detailed as possible.

Don't forget to consult with your advisors. Tax laws are always changing, and it is wise to update your estate plan at least once a year and meet with your team of advisors on a regular basis. It will cost you some money, but good advice will save you much more in the long run.

TIPS FOR HEIRS: This is another chapter that can benefit you only if others read and heed it. You can, however, discuss the relevant issues with your loved ones and share it with them when it seems appropriate. Good communication between family members often avoids the pitfalls of estate planning and eases the transfer of assets. Involvement in a parent's collecting activities may create new and lasting bonds between the family members; you may even begin to enjoy collecting yourself.

CARL LAEMMLE
presents

FRANKENSTEIN
THE MAN WHO MADE A MONSTER

with
COLIN CLIVE
MAE CLARKE
JOHN BOLES
BORIS KARLOFF
DWIGHT FRYE · EDWARD VAN SLOAN
and FREDERIC KERR
Based upon the MARY WOLLSTONECRAFT
SHELLEY STORY
Adapted by JOHN L. BALDERSTON *from*
the play by PEGGY WEBLING

Frankenstein (Universal, 1931).
Three Sheet (41" X 78.5") Style C.
Sold for: $358,500 | March 2015

Directed by JAMES WHALE
Produced by CARL LAEMMLE JR.
A UNIVERSAL PICTURE

43

Mark Prendergast's Story

Mark Prendergast is the Director of Trusts & Estates at Heritage Auctions, working out of the company's Houston office to provide assistance to fiduciary professionals and estate executors throughout the country. Prior to joining Heritage, he worked as a dealer of 20th century American Art and as a Christie's Vice President.

Estate planning has ramifications that extend far beyond money. Even the most benevolent plans can lead to irreparable family strife, and the best intentions can backfire badly when the unanticipated happens due to fluctuating markets.

In the early 2000s, I was working on the estate tax appraisal of a husband-wife team of collectors who had passed away in short succession. The bulk of their collection was left to local museums, but their son and daughter had each been left a painting that they had especially liked. The daughter inherited a gorgeous 19th century English Orientalist work, and the son received a 1960s work by the Pop Artist Ed Ruscha; both were appraised at about $250,000. They had asked for the paintings because they enjoyed them but, as is often the case, the allure of the money was too much to resist and within a year, both works came up for auction.

If you remember the art market of the early 2000s, you can probably guess what happened next. The market for Pop Art went on a tear, and the market for 19th century Orientalism had its ups and downs. The daughter's piece sold above its auction estimate for $340,000, but the son's 1960s painting — which had carried the same appraised value and comparable auction estimate — Sold for: $1.1 million. The million dollars the son took home created major problems in his relationship with his sister, something that the parents had, no doubt, never intended when they were planning for their estate. The son predictably felt that the distribution had been equitable — that his piece had simply appreciated in value more than anyone would have anticipated — and the daughter, also understandably, felt that she had been treated unfairly. Had the parents simply sold the works during their lifetime — or directed the estate to sell the works — and then divided the proceeds evenly, each heir could have received $720,000 (less commissions) and family holidays would have remained a pleasant affair.

The point of this story? If your goal is equitable distribution to multiple heirs, consider selling your collection during your lifetime, or directing the estate to liquidate the collection and divvy up the cash. It lacks the romance of letting heirs pick their favorite pieces, but remember that a seemingly emotional attachment to an object often has financial undertones. The market for antiques, fine art, and collectibles is too unpredictable to divide up collections without a very real risk of inequity, and inequity can lead to family strife.

Fr. 379b $1000 1890 Treasury Note PCGS
Extremely Fine 40.
Sold for: $3,290,000 | January 2014

6

Should You Bequeath Your Collection, or Sell During Your Lifetime?

"The main thing is to be moved, to love, to hope, to tremble, to live."
– Auguste Rodin

A collector spends countless hours of life carefully and lovingly amassing a collection, often having fought for individual pieces at auctions, made great discoveries in unlikely locales, overpaid for that much needed example and watched as the value of that collection grew over the years. But ultimately it is the collector's (and maybe also the spouse's) collection – and unfortunately we don't regularly see the same appreciation or passion in other members of the family or heirs. To sell a collection during the collector's lifetime can provide for enjoyment, accolades and the benefit of reaping the financial rewards. That financial realization can be used for donations, gifts or to pursue building a better collection – or beginning in a whole new collecting field.

We, as collectors ourselves, understand the fun of collecting and the pleasure to be found in the thrill of the hunt. We see many collectors who sell an entire collection multiple times during their lives and then branch into very variant directions of interest – or choose to concentrate their collecting to much higher quality examples in their field.

We will touch on the applicable tax implication a bit later, and a more detailed explanation of various taxes are discussed later in this book, but first, let's consider some of the logistical and practical reasons for selling a collection during one's lifetime rather than donating, gifting or leaving the collection in your estate.

Unlike most of our heirs, most collectors know what prices we paid and what sort of profit (or loss) we can reasonably expect. We follow the market and know when it might be a good time to sell – and conversely when it looks to be more of a "buyer's market." We like to know our collection is represented accurately during the sale process, offered for sale in the best possible market venue and that we are getting a good price for our pieces.

A collector may have established relationships with a particular auction house or dealer – or at least have strong opinions as to what venue they would prefer to see their collection sold through. Being able to make the decision of sale venue and negotiate the best possible sale terms should be the responsibility and concern of the collector themselves – and not left as a burden to their heirs. All too often we see situations where inherited collections or disinterested families sell in inadequate local venues or to unscrupulous dealers and receive only a small percentage of the true value.

> *Recently, Heritage's Trusts & Estates Department was approached by an heir who had inherited half of his father's comic book collection and wanted to know what the sale potential and market value was for his inheritance. The comics turned out to be wonderful examples of some rare and excellent condition Golden and Silver Age comic from the 1940s through 1960s. Heritage marketed the collection extensively and ended up selling the comics at auction for over $800,000. When we asked the heir about the other half of the collection that had been left to his sibling, he told us the all too familiar story of the other half having been sold locally for less than $15,000. His sibling's disinterest and lack of knowledge about the value potential for the collection resulted in a significant loss of inheritance. Surely not their father's intention.*

Though will codicils and directives may be written to instruct your heirs as to how you would prefer your collection to be dispersed or sold as part of your estate (email Estates@HA.com for sample documents), those directives are not always fully enforceable or followed. By overseeing the sale themselves, collectors know that they have done best for their collection and are able to receive the recognition and value so deserved.

To Gift or not to Gift

If a collection is valued over the current lifetime gift tax or estate tax exemption threshold ($5.45 million in 2016) or the combined assets of an individual exceed that amount, then it is important to consider the implications of paying estate tax upon your passing versus possible gift tax during your lifetime. There are very practical tax benefits of selling high value items or collections during your lifetime rather than just allowing your estate and heirs to deal with the distribution, sale and taxes.

As per the American Taxpayer Act of 2013 (ATRA), the lifetime gift tax exemption matches the federal estate tax exemption and will increase over the years to account for inflation. The lifetime gift tax and estate tax exemption was raised for 2016 to $5.45 million per taxpayer with a taxable rate of 40% for gift tax or estate tax over the exemption amount. Gifts at or under the $14,000 per recipient yearly exclusion ($28,000 per recipient per married couple) do not encroach on the lifetime gift tax exemption, but gift amounts over the allowed exclusion will be deducted from the lifetime exemption and will also then reduce the estate tax exemption for that individual. For example, a married couple with two married children and four grandchildren could gift $28,000 to each of their eight heirs for $224,000 in annual gifts that are tax exempt and do not apply to their lifetime gift tax exemption.

Another benefit of lifetime gifting is that by making the gift of a tangible item, you are establishing a new cost basis as of the date of the gift for the fair market value. The recipients, whether a trust or individual, would then benefit from less capital gains taxes when they choose to sell. Again, the particulars of all types of tax rates and implications are discussed later in this book.

A collector may want to consider the benefits of the gift tax as an alternative to capital gains and the estate tax. Here is an example situation for individuals with high value collections and net worth, though as we repeatedly express throughout this book, it is very important to consult with your accountant or tax professional as to each individual's specific situations.

If a collector and their spouse/partner were to gift a $20 million coin collection to their six heirs (children and grandchildren or their trusts) over the course of five years, deducting the $10.9 million lifetime gift tax exemption for the couple and the yearly gift tax exclusions, they would pay the gift tax at 40% on just $8.26 million, which would be $3.3 million in tax paid from their other assets. The heirs would receive the full $20 million of the collection. Then the coins would have the benefit of a stepped-up basis of value of $20 million as of the date of the gift. If the heirs then sold the collection at auction, say in 5 years after the gift, for $30 million – they would pay the capital gains tax on the $10 million of gained value. At the 28% long term capital gain tax rate for coins and collectibles – the tax due would be $2.8 million – netting them $27.2 million free and clear.

Now if our couple's coin collection was held until they both passed - say in that same 5 year period – and sold by their estate for the $30 million, the heirs would see a net total of only $24 million after the 40% estate. That is an extra $3.2 million for their heirs from a bit of advanced planning. Those same assets ($20 million in coins and $5.5 in other assets), if sold at auction by the estate during the same time frame for the same $30 million sale result, would net the family $35.5 million minus 40% estate tax after the estate tax exemption of $5.43 million, for a total of just $23.5 million, almost $4 million less after taxes than if the coins had been gifted to the family members rather than left in the estate.

The family, either directly or via a trust, would be better off financially by taking ownership of the coins now. Also, that would allow the collector the option to actually advise and oversee the sale through auction. This is a simple example; every situation will have a multitude of variables and considerations of estate planning, which should be discussed with your tax professional.

Donation Considerations

The notion of preserving one's legacy for future generations, alongside other treasures of the world in the protected confines of museums, libraries and archives, is a nice altruistic concept.

Unfortunately, the reality of what actually will happen to your beloved collection upon donation may not reflect your intent and expectations.

Museums and non-profit institutions may or may not have the need or desire for your beloved collection. As we discuss in the chapter on charitable giving, in order for the collector to receive the maximum tax benefits of a donation, the receiving entity must have "related and like use" of the items. Even if accepted for donation, the item may find its way to the museum's storage cabinets and racks never to see the glory of public display. A collector's perception of the importance of works of art or collectibles may not be shared by the current or future curator or the mission and direction of a museum can change over the years.

A museum's permanent collection is not always permanent and museums are a consistent source of material in the auction market. Whether sold to fund future acquisitions, assist with the wider capital campaigns, or even provide operating funds, institutions often have a more pressing need for money than objects. In many cases, it is much preferred for an institution to receive a cash donation over someone's collection. Selling items or a collection through auction with the specific catalog notation that the pieces are to be sold to benefit a certain charitable entity holds the added possible benefits of state sales tax exemption and tax exemptions for the buyer which will generate more interest from bidders and higher sale prices.

Also donating the proceeds of the sale of an item often doesn't carry the same concerns of Internal Revenue Service scrutiny as does an appraised valuation. In many, if not most instances, an auction sale is the very definition of fair market value - which is what a charitable donation valuation must reflect. Past abuses, including outright fraud and tax evasion, have led to very strict requirements for acceptable charitable donation appraisals, which are more fully explained in a the appraisal chapter of this book.

Many institutions will not accept donations that are bound by stipulations of permanent holding or display. In the end, most non-profit institutions have more use for monetary gifts than tangible assets. Only a very small percentage of donated items actually get displayed.

Furthermore, when a particular painting or artifact becomes especially valuable in the market, the decision may be made to sell it in order to obtain the monetary funds which could support much more important endeavors then filling up a small part of one wall in a museum. Quite often, museums, finding themselves in desperate need of funds, end up in court disputing the very agreements they signed with long-deceased donors decades earlier.

If the institution is requesting the gift or donation from you, the object probably has a much better chance of regular exhibition – though there is never a long-term guarantee. If the donated item is regularly displayed, it will usually have acknowledgement of the source of the donation on the wall plaque and in any published literature. You can receive the same recognition, which also benefits the item by providing an exhibition history, by loaning items for periods of time or considering a fractional gift. Including art or collectibles as part of museum exhibitions adds to the provenance or history of a piece which will make it just that much more desirable and valuable to the market.

Auctioning a collection in its entirety can increase the value of the lesser pieces in the collection by association with the most sought after pieces. By establishing a collection identity, the provenance and pedigree of that collection will carry forth with the items for evermore to add addition recognition and appreciation both for your name and the items. Especially in the collectible categories such as coins and comic books, the importance of a famous or well-known pedigree can truly increase value of an item. Also in the areas of art and jewelry, pieces from well-respected collections carry added mystique and interest in the market.

The thought of parting with a beloved collection may seem initially unwelcomed and unthinkable, but the fact is that the 'letting go' of a collection is an inevitable as part of a collector's life - the question is how and when. With proper planning, making wise decisions to oversee and control the sale, gift or donation can lead to greater after-tax monetary reward, family harmony and fulfilling charitable objectives.

A Decision to Sell ·············· The Gardner Collection

When it comes to selling a collection that was assembled over years as a labor of love, many collectors like to have a hand in the process, using the sale as a way to document their connection to the items under their care and to share the stories behind them.

In total, the over 3,000 coins in the collection of Pennsylvania collector Eugene H. Gardner brought more than $53 million across four major auctions at Heritage between 2014 and 2015.

The collection was the product of a keen eye and a passion for numismatics that began in 1954 when as a college student Gardner began assembling his first coin collection. That collection was sold in 1965 but Gardner soon caught the collecting bug again. The resulting "second collection" was widely considered by numismatic experts to be among the finest collections of silver coinage ever assembled. Gardner said he learned many lessons when putting together his first collection, applying these in his second collecting effort.

For Gardner, it was important for him to work with Heritage in the presentation of his collection as he viewed the auctions as the culmination of a gratifying and absorbing collecting career. Gardner said that the sale of his collection, "allows me to introduce my largely-completed collection to the numismatic fraternity, which is very exciting to me. I love the thought of sharing the auction experience with my family. We've really all been in this together. In fact, my grandchildren know how to get my attention by just saying, 'Opa, what new coins do you have?'"

A Decision to Sell ⋯⋯⋯⋯⋯⋯⋯⋯⋯⋯⋯⋯⋯⋯

The Gardner Collection

His decision to sell his collection across a series of Heritage sales during the course of a year rather than a single auction served multiple purposes – all in the interest of maximizing the sale totals. First, it allowed collectors and dealers to stretch out their bidding dollars instead of having to use all of their funds at one time. Second, the strategy allowed key parts of the collector's groups of early U.S. silver coins, Barber coins and Seated Liberty material to be spread out fairly evenly. Gardner purchased many of his coins at auction, making the prices that he paid public record – so by establishing a new price point would allow for even higher prices in the subsequent auctions.

Looking at the results of the Gardner sales shows that many coins went up in value, a few went down, and some went unchanged in their trips to the auction block. A collection's success at auction needs to be looked at as a whole, because at auction, anything can happen with a single lot. Success is best measured by how well a collection does in total for the collection as a whole.

Gardner's 1802 Draped Bust half dime, graded an About Uncirculated 50, was a highlight. As Heritage's catalog noted, "One of the most desirable coins in high grade in the Gardner Collection, the 1802 half dime is a signal rarity, a 'trophy coin' for even the most advanced numismatist and an issue unknown in Mint State."

It had sold at a 2009 Heritage auction for $195,500 (then graded by the Professional Coin Grading Service as an Extremely Fine 45). At the first Gardner auction on June 23, 2014, the piece (upgraded to an About Uncirculated 50) sold for a strong $352,500, that price serving as a testament to the quality and rarity of the piece. Heritage worked with Gardner to help maximize value in his collection, seeking upgrades when possible. The result was that Gardner – and his legacy as a collector – will survive for generations in the many coins that carry the Gardner pedigree.

**Prince Owned And Played Custom Made
Signature Yellow Cloud Guitar (Circa 1988-1994).**
Sold for: $137,500 | June 2016

7

Tax Options for Estate Planning

"The only difference between death and taxes is that death doesn't get worse every time Congress meets." – Will Rogers

If you are an avid collector, your collection may represent a large portion of your net worth and your estate. While your real estate, stocks, bonds, and other traditional investments are probably accounted for in your estate plan, your collection may not be. The only way that your advisor will know that you have a collection is if you share that information with her. Even if it is an approximate value, your advisor will consider these assets in the planning process.

When a person dies owning property, that property is transferred to a recipient. The process of determining the recipients of those assets—who gets what and what will be done about taxes—is the central purpose of estate planning. The decisions you make can have a significant impact on the amount of ordinary income, capital gains, gift and/or estate taxes that you or your heirs will pay. This chapter is provided to improve your general understanding, as we cannot know or advise you as to which of these options may apply to your personal situation or holdings.

We strongly recommend that, after studying this information, you engage the services of a competent legal professional, preferably an attorney who is board-certified in estate planning and/or probate law by your state, and a tax advisor, preferably a CPA. An experienced and competent professional with expertise in life insurance should also become a valuable part of your team of advisors.

Between you and your advisory team, you should be able to create the plan that best suits your unique needs and wishes. Tax and estate planning laws can be extremely complex and there is no single individual who can be relied upon to advise you on all aspects of the legal, tax and insurance matters that are involved in estate planning. As we stated before, tax laws are always changing and have significant impact on the taxation of your estate, and on decisions about the benefits and detriments of making lifetime gifts, or gifts by will or trust. For example, long-term capital gains on collectibles are currently taxed at a rate of 28% or your marginal tax rate, whichever is lower, while long-term capital gains on other assets, like your stocks or real estate, are generally taxed at a lower rate of 15%.

Annual gifts of up to $14,000 (since 2013) may be made by you to as many individuals as you choose without affecting your lifetime gift exemption. If your wife joins you in the gift, you can distribute $28,000 each year to as many lucky recipients as you choose, without reducing your joint lifetime exemption. In addition, as of 2016, you are allowed a $5,450,000 lifetime gift exemption, ($10,900,000 with your spouse/partner), and a generous gift tax exemption for generation-skipping gifts to grandchildren. For future years, the lifetime gift tax exemption will be increased for inflation each year with the tax rate remaining at 40%.

Is Your Collection Worth More Today Than When You Purchased It?

As with any carefully chosen investment, a collection should hopefully appreciate in value over time. There are, of course, exceptions.

If you were unfortunate enough to have been the victim of an unscrupulous seller, or perhaps acquired some of your collectibles at the peak of a market that has since declined, a current appraisal may indicate that you are in a capital loss position. If that's the case, you may sell the collection and use the loss to offset an equal amount of capital gains. In addition, you may deduct up to $3,000 annually ($1,500 if you are married and filing separately) of excess capital losses against your ordinary income. These losses may be carried forward to future years until they are entirely used, or until your death.

Certain losses, depending on their character (short- or long-term) may offset only certain gains and the IRS has established a priority for offsetting short- and long-term capital gains. The best strategy when you incur capital gains that can't be offset with losses is to simply pay the tax. If the collection has appreciated, many other issues come into play. These are discussed over the next few pages.

The Unpredictability of the Estate Tax

Unless you have successfully completed your lifetime planning, many of the assets held directly in your name will transfer into your estate upon your death. Your estate will have to pay estate taxes if the net value is greater than the exemption size set by Congress. Unfortunately, Congress has made planning for the estate tax challenging by continually changing the size of the exemptions. The American Tax Relief Act of 2013 set the estate tax exemption threshold at $5,340,000 per tax payer for 2014 and will be indexed for inflation each year. 2015 now sees the exemption at $5,430,000 and in 2016 the exemption rose to $5,450,000. Beginning January 1, 2011, estates of decedents survived by a spouse may elect to pass any of the decedent's unused exemption to the surviving spouse. Some states have estate tax provisions as well and should also be considered during estate planning.

This is all very confusing, but the consequences of the estate tax are important. If you bequeath a large estate of tangible assets to your heirs, without proper planning, your heirs may require a substantial amount of liquid money to satisfy the estate taxes. If there is no estate tax in the year of the estate (as happened in 2010 and 2011) they may still have to pay significant capital gains taxes if items are sold, as the cost basis of the property would not have been re-established and updated in filings as part of the estate.

Without extensions, estate taxes must be paid to the government in cash within nine months of death. Often, the unfortunate result of this immediate need for cash will be a "fire sale" to raise the required funds by the tax filing date. A hasty sale will not maximize the value of the collection you have devoted a great amount of time and effort to. Despite your best intentions, your heirs may not benefit from your collection as you had intended without proper planning.

Julian Onderdonk (American, 1882-1922)
Texas Landscape with Bluebonnets
Oil on canvas
25 x 30 inches
Sold for: $437,000 | November 2015

One part of the solution to the need of immediate liquidity to pay for potential estate taxes can be life insurance.

First, you will need your accountant or advisor to develop a pro forma balance sheet and income statement to determine the extent of the potential tax liability based upon the best estimate of the value of your estate at some unknown date. Depending on the valuation of your estate, your advisor can estimate the amount of tax that may be due upon your passing.

This part of your planning is more of an art than a science. The value of your assets, which may appreciate or depreciate over time, is somewhat unpredictable. Because one's date of death is uncertain, the tax rates that will apply are uncertain. There are many unknowns, but you have to work with what you have. As Yogi Berra put it, "Predictions, especially about the future, are hard to make." Your advisor, based on these assumptions, should be able to assist you in determining the tax consequences of making lifetime gifts compared with making bequests at the time of your passing as directed in your estate plan. These assumptions will also determine the various strategies that are available to reduce your tax liabilities.

The amount of life insurance required to pay the estimated tax should be determined in consultation with an insurance advisor as well as your estate planning attorney.

A life insurance policy's proceeds do not become part of your estate at death as long as you do not name either yourself or your estate as the beneficiary of the policy; placing the ownership of the policy in a separate trust (an irrevocable life insurance trust, or ILIT for short) outside of your estate or owned by a third party is one good approach. The proceeds of the policy are payable immediately in cash and pass to your beneficiaries income tax-free. By insuring your life for an amount equal to or in excess of your estimated estate tax liability, you can assure your heirs of sufficient liquidity to pay the estate taxes, thus enabling the collection to pass to your heirs without requiring them to sell assets. If they choose to sell assets, they won't have any tax liability to worry about and will be able to maximize value by selling in an orderly fashion without government- imposed deadlines. This is discussed in more detail in a later chapter.

The Gift Tax and Reducing Your Estate through Annual Gifting

Especially in light of the onerous estate tax rates that can inflict substantial damage on your estate (remember that potential tax rate of 40%), reducing your taxable estate through gifts to your heirs during your lifetime is a simple and extremely advantageous strategy, if implemented properly. This is where you need to understand the gift tax.

The gift tax applies to transfers of assets during your lifetime to various recipients. Current law allows you to make gifts of present interest to any number of recipients. The donor is responsible for the payment of any taxes that are due on the gift. In general, a gift is a transfer of property for less than its full value.

A gift must be accepted by the recipient and is irrevocable. As previously discussed, our current tax law provides for annual gifts of $14,000 per recipient (for 2016). If your spouse participates in the gift, you are allowed to give away $28,000 per year to as many fortunate individuals as you wish. If your gift does not exceed that amount, you do not even have to fill out a tax form for these annual gifts. However, there are limitations. You are also entitled to a one-time lifetime gift tax exemption of $5,450,000 per spouse in 2016. Certain gifts are not considered taxable gifts, including medical and educational expenses that you pay for someone, gifts to your spouse and gifts to a political organization for its use. Once you exceed the annual gift tax limitation of $14,000 per individual, or $28,000 with spouse, two things will happen: You will be required to report the gift to the IRS and it will reduce your lifetime gift tax exemptions dollar for dollar. If you exceed the $5.45 million or $10.9 million dollar limitation, you may be subject to the 40% estate tax.

In theory, if you have 10 children and grandchildren (in total), you and your spouse may gift up to $280,000 ($28,000 times 10) each year to them without filing with the IRS. More good things will result. Not only will you make these family members very happy, you will have removed $280,000 from your estate, which is no longer subject to future appreciation and possible estate taxation.

Those who make gifts on a regular annual basis can substantially reduce their estate tax liabilities as long as there are a sufficient number of recipients to make gifts to. Using the above example, in 10 years, it is possible to eliminate $2.8 million from your estate without affecting your lifetime gift tax exemption.

What are the benefits of making gifts as compared to disposing of your assets by will or trust upon your death?

First, there is no downside in using your annual gift tax exemptions as long as it does not deplete your financial resources.

Why would you use the $5.45 million lifetime exemption—$10.9 million with your spouse—rather than wait until you pass away and use your estate tax exemptions? The primary reason is that if you use the exemptions to gift property that may appreciate substantially in future years, you will eliminate any future appreciation in these assets from your estate—thus rendering them untouched by the estate tax.

For example, let's say you decide to make a lifetime gift to your daughter of a painting with a fair market value of $5,000,000. When you pass away, many years from now, the painting is worth $8,000,000. You have reduced your taxable estate (again, think 40% and possibly more in the future) by $3 million. By making the gift early, you could potentially save over a million dollars in estate taxes.

If the same painting is in your estate when you die and is not a gift, the recipient receives what is known as a stepped-up basis in the asset. Basically, if the recipient decides to sell the asset, the basis for determining their gain is determined by the value of the property at the time of your death, which eliminates most of the tax liability if the property is sold soon after you pass away. The problem is that if you retain the property in your estate when you die, you will be subject to the 40% estate tax.

Gifted property usually has what is called a carryover basis. The amount used to determine the gain to the recipient is the original cost of the asset, not the value of the asset at the time of the gift. So let's say you acquired the painting years ago and have a cost basis of $1,000,000, but the current fair market value of $5,000,000. If you give it to your daughter now, there will be a capital gain of $4,000,000 ($5,000,000, minus $1,000,000) waiting for her if she decides to sell it. This could be eliminated if the property remains in your estate and your assets do not exceed the exemptions.

Under current law - and we emphasize current law as things may change soon as an election year - you may gift an unlimited amount of property during your lifetime to a spouse without paying gift tax as long as your marriage is legally recognized and your spouse is a U.S. citizen. Upon your death, the marital deduction allows you to pass an unlimited amount of property to your spouse tax-free. It should be noted that marital transfers merely defer estate taxes; they do not eliminate them. However, using the marital deduction to equalize the estates of both spouses will allow you to maximize your estate tax exemptions, by transferring assets between the two of you. For federal tax purposes, the terms "spouse," "husband," and "wife" includes individuals of the same-sex who were lawfully married under the laws of a state whose laws authorize the marriage of two individuals of the same sex and who remain married.

The use of annual and lifetime gifts is an essential part of any estate plan. It's not exciting, but it is important. At a minimum, you now have a basic understanding of the concepts to enable you to ask the appropriate questions of your advisors.

At the risk of being repetitive, let's summarize the basic concepts, in the simplest of terms, with the caveat that nothing in this area is simple and legislation is pending that could change many of these rates.

You have a $14,000 annual gift tax exemption that permits gifts to unlimited recipients each year, or $28,000 per year if your spouse joins you. Use this gift to reduce the size of your estate, eliminate the appreciation of assets in your estate, and enjoy the benefits of generosity—if that sort of thing appeals to you. If you have property in your estate that will appreciate, consider using your lifetime gift tax exemption of $5.45 million, or $10.9 million with your spouse, assuming you are financially comfortable without the asset. If your estate is estimated at a value that may trigger the estate tax, one should consider the use of a life insurance trust and a charitable remainder trust (which we'll discuss a little later) to minimize potential taxation. The recipient may incur higher taxes upon the receipt and sale of a gift from you than would be the case if the property was received upon death and sold soon afterwards. There are, though, other strategies to reduce those potential liabilities as well.

Fractional Gifting Considerations

Collectors who own very valuable collections, or certain pieces of art/collectibles that well exceed the $14,000 tax exempt annual gift allowance, and wish to reduce their taxable estates, may consider the use of fractional gifting over time, either directly or through establishing beneficiary Trusts. Gifting a percentage of the ownership--and thus value--of an item allows for the retention of the piece by the collector while still lowering the taxable estate to more manageable and advantageous amounts each year. A $14,000 fractional gift to a few family members annually may equal just a small percentage of the value of an object or collection, but over a number of years or even decades, if planning begins early, collectors can make full use of their tax exempt gift allowances.

The Capital Gains Tax and Like-Kind Exchanges

Everything you own for investment purposes is a capital asset. This includes any investment properties you have, stocks and bonds, mutual funds, and collections—if you bought them with an eye toward investment.

When you sell a capital asset, the difference between the price you paid for it (known as your cost basis) and the amount you sell it for is a capital gain or capital loss.

If you held the asset for more than a year before selling, it is considered long term. If you held the asset for less than a year, it is short term.

DAVID HAMMONS (American, b. 1943)
Feed Folks, 1974
Mixed media
39-3/4 x 29-1/2 inches
Sold for: $1,205,000 | May 2014

The cost basis of an asset depends upon how you acquired the asset. If you purchased the asset, the basis is the amount you paid at the time of purchase, including but not limited to any associated expenses, such as commissions, fees, and improvements to the property, etc. If you received the property as a gift, the basis is usually the price that the donor making the gift originally paid for it, which is also called the "carryover basis." If you inherited the asset upon the death of the donor, your basis is the fair market value of the asset at the date of death, called a "stepped-up basis."

For example, if you are a collector who paid $10,000 for a collection, and at your death the collection is worth $50,000, whoever inherits your collection will have a stepped-up basis of $50,000. The effect is to eliminate the $40,000 in gains that you would have incurred. However, you have to die for the gain to be erased—perhaps a high price to pay for some tax savings. Also, the asset that has appreciated will be included in the value of your estate at the appreciated value, not the original cost.

Capital gains on most assets held for more than one year are taxed at a lower rate than ordinary income. The capital gains tax is generally 15% on most assets, other than collectibles, that have been held for a year or more. However, the long-term capital gains on the sale of collectibles—such as coins, stamps, precious gems, precious metals and rare currency or fine art—are taxed at a maximum rate of 28%. If your marginal income tax rate is below 28%, your gain on the sale of collectibles will be taxed at the marginal rate; if your marginal rate is above 28%, your gain will be taxed at 28%—providing you with some tax savings, but not nearly what you'd get with investments in stocks or bonds. Short term gains on objects sold within a one-year time frame are taxed at the same rate as your ordinary income tax rate (this is true for all investments—from stocks and bonds to more obscure collectible investments).

Even the most astute of advisors may not be aware of the exception for long-term capital gains that applies only to collectibles. The consequences of this tax, and its application to collectibles, are critical as there are a number of strategies that may be available to reduce the pain. Do not be deceived by those who may tell you that the tax is only 15% or less.

One strategy to defer long-term capital gains taxes on your collectible is to use a Section 1031 like-kind exchange. With this, the tax is not eliminated, but deferred. While a 1031 exchange is commonly used with real estate, it is also applicable to art and other collectibles. The IRS has specifically addressed coins and Section 1031 exchanges and it may be used to defer payment of long-term capital gains tax into the future. Only at such time as the replacement property is sold, will the capital gains tax become due. The requirements for these exchanges are extremely technical, but three basic elements are required by the taxing authorities to comply with the regulations:

1. There is an exchange of property that qualifies under Section 1031.

2. The properties exchanged are like-kind to one another.

3. Both properties are held for investment, or used productively in a trade or business.

The first element is clear, but the second one addressing like-kind is more challenging. Like-kind refers to the nature or character of the property, and not its grade or quality.

For example, the IRS has ruled that collectible coins are not like-kind to bullion coins, and that gold bullion is not like-kind to silver bullion. The IRS makes the distinction that the value of numismatic-type coins is determined by their age, the quantity minted, along with history, art and aesthetics, condition, and finally, metal content. On the other hand, the value of bullion coins such as the popular South African Krugerrands is determined solely on the basis of their metal content.

The third element, "held for investment," means that the property was held primarily for profit. The burden of proof falls on the collector to prove that he invested in his collection with the goal of making a profit.

The key to all of this is documentation. The IRS will determine the investment purpose by examining your past records. How frequently do you buy and sell your collectibles? What is the profit motive? How much time do you devote to reading catalogs and other materials that enhance your knowledge and investment savvy? Do you travel to shows to gain knowledge of the market or to pursue your hobby? Do you own the type of collectibles that are likely to appreciate? Are the purchases of rare or common pieces? If you are purchasing common objects, it will be difficult to demonstrate to the IRS that you are an investor and not a hobbyist (of course, if you are purchasing common objects, a 1031 exchange will likely be more trouble than it's worth). It is essential to document all your activities that will support the argument that you purchased your collectibles with the intention of future price appreciation.

While the concept behind 1031 exchanges is fairly straightforward, the specific rules involving Section 1031 exchanges are more complicated.

Sellers have 45 days to identify their replacement property, and then 180 days to complete the purchase of the new property. If you miss the deadline, the tax break is forfeited. Additionally, the IRS requires that an exchanger use a "qualified intermediary," or a middleman. The purpose of a "QI" is to hold the proceeds of the sale in escrow until the new property is purchased.

The QI is one of four parties in a typical tax-deferred exchange. The second is the taxpayer who has property and wants to exchange it for new property. The third is the seller who owns the property that the taxpayer wants to acquire in the exchange. The final party is the buyer who has cash and wants to acquire the taxpayer's property.

Section 1031 exchanges may be a useful tool to defer capital gains taxes when a collection is sold. However, it is essential that a collector receive qualified tax advice and comply with all of the regulations in this area. There is currently legislation before Congress that would exclude collectibles from inclusion in the 1031 exchange, but it has not had any success to this point.

A final warning: Do not proceed without expert tax advice, as there may be other strategies that may be preferable alternatives to the like-kind exchange. Remember, taxes are deferred, not eliminated, and there are substantial costs involved in a 1031 exchange regarding fees and other costs. Also, there is always the possibility that the property you receive in the exchange will lose value, while the property that you sell may appreciate. 1031 exchanges should only be considered for properties of high value; on lower-end deals, the costs of the 1031 exchange will quickly outstrip any tax savings.

Trusts

The most commonly used trust is the living trust. In legal terms, it is known as the "revocable living trust." In simple terms, the living trust is a document that is used in conjunction with a Will, but avoids the costs and time involved in probating a Will. You transfer your property and title it in the name of the trust; for example, you might be John Doe, trustee for the John Doe Trust.

Of course, you will need a competent estate planning attorney to draft the documents and explain them to you. A trust is advised for both you and your spouse. A Will is only a supplement to the trust that will assure that any assets that have not been transferred into your trust (re-titled) will shift into the trust at the time of your death. Remember, only assets that have been re-titled in the name of the trust will be valid transfers that will accomplish your objectives.

While you are alive, you may be the trustee of your own trust and maintain complete control of the assets. When you pass away, the trustee(s) you select becomes the new trustee. The new trustee, called a successor trustee, has a fiduciary obligation to follow the terms of the trust as you have stated in the trust document.

A revocable trust, in itself, will not result in specific tax savings. But the advantages are important: While the terms of a Will are public knowledge, the terms of a trust are private, and within the control of you and the parties that you select to be involved in the process. Assets will be transferred soon after death, legal fees will be minimized and the terms will remain private. Also, there is far less risk of an unhappy family member contesting a trust than a Will.

There may be ancillary tax benefits. The trust will provide for the disposition of your assets in accordance with your wishes. In addition, the trust will permit you to take full advantage of the marital deduction and your tax exemptions by designating the exact proportion of assets to be distributed to which recipients.

This is a summary only and an expert is required to properly draft the trust and other ancillary documents. One of the other major benefits of a living trust is that it can contain directions for the trustee as to your care, and the protection of your assets, should you be unable to make such decisions due to your health or mental condition. Your designated trustee will assume control of your property and make the necessary decisions—which is a better option than putting a judge in control of your assets.

There is also an AB trust, commonly called a QTIP (Qualified Terminable Interest Property), bypass trust or a marital trust, where spouses leave property in trust for their children, but provide the surviving spouse with the right to use the property or income from the property for his or her lifetime. The AB trust maximizes the deceased spouse's personal exemption (currently that aforementioned $5,450,000 in 2016). The result, if properly executed, is the ability to take full advantage of the total of $10,900,000 of estate exemptions allowed to both spouses based on the current tax law exemption for 2016.

A QTIP trust permits a spouse to transfer assets to their trust while maintaining control over the disposition of those assets upon the death of the spouse. These trusts are common in second marriages where a person desires assurance that the children from the first marriage will receive assets which could conceivably go to children from the second marriage. Irrevocable life insurance trusts are often used because life insurance proceeds are not taxable unless the ownership of the policies is in your name or the estate is the beneficiary of the policy. You can transfer a small amount, equal to the life insurance premium, to an irrevocable life insurance trust through your heirs and use of your annual gifts, which will reduce the size of your taxable estate while creating a much larger asset (the life insurance proceeds) that remains outside of the estate.

As an heir to a taxable estate, once the donor or owner of the collectible has passed away, most of your opportunities to reduce the estate tax consequences will have passed. It can be awkward, but if you're worried that a parent or anyone else you are likely to inherit property from has not been engaging the right advisors for estate planning, you may be able to advise them to meet with an advisor. This approach—suggesting meeting with advisors to make sure that everything is in accordance with their wishes—is preferable to making the conversation more specific.

If it is necessary to liquidate all or part of the collection to pay estate taxes, the expenses of that liquidation (shipping, insurance, auction fees, commissions, etc.) are generally deductible from the estate. Additionally, estate expenses related to the use of lawyers and probate costs are deductible from the total gross estate. It is still advantageous to arrange your estate plan to reduce these expenses rather than to deduct them (see living trust).

If you are the surviving spouse of the deceased, exemptions generally allow the estate to pass to you without taxes being owed. The estate planning burden then becomes yours, however, as the same exemptions will not apply at your death unless you remarry. If this eventuality was not already considered in your planning, you should contact an estate or tax professional without delay. Even if the survivor's estate issues were considered in the original planning, it cannot hurt to reevaluate the situation with a trusted advisor.

Life Insurance and Taxes

"Helpful self-test questionnaire to see if you have enough life insurance (Sponsored by the Life Insurance Institute): 1.) How much life insurance do you have? ___ 2.) You need more. 3.) We'll send somebody over right now." – Dave Barry

Although most of us have certain suspicions regarding insurance advisors, the truth is that life insurance is one of the most valuable tools available under our current tax structure—when it's integrated holistically into financial planning with the advice of a competent professional who is focused on more than the size of the commission check. Many insurance specialists are well-trained and are experts in their fields. If you're concerned about self-dealing and an agent who may be incentivized to steer you into a policy that benefits the

A. Lange & Söhne, Glashütte,
Extremely Fine & Rare Ref. 701.005
Platinum Tourbillon "Pour le Mérite"
No. 42 of a limited edition of 50
examples made in 1996
Sold for: $245,000 | November 2014

salesman more than the purchaser, consider dealing through a fee-only financial advisor who specializes in insurance or, as some financial advisors now recommend, a fee-only life insurance consultant.

Life insurance is afforded a number of tax advantages that are unavailable with other forms of investments. It is highly leveraged and if you die after the initial premium has been paid, you will receive a large multiple of that amount in cash.

An expert insurance advisor is a critical component of your estate planning team. Ideally, long-term life insurance should be purchased while you are young and healthy. The same benefits may not be available should you become ill or incapacitated. Do not wait until you are in poor health, or when you are at such an age that the costs of insurance are prohibitive.

There are two primary purposes for life insurance in planning for estates substantial enough to incur taxation at the maximum rate.

The first is liquidity. Life insurance must be held outside of your estate. The IRS will want its money right away, and the liquidity provided by a life insurance payout may allow you to avoid having to sell your collections at "fire sale" prices. Remember, not all insurance proceeds are excluded from your estate: If you are the owner of the policy or you name either yourself or your estate as the beneficiary, the proceeds will be included in the valuation of your estate upon death. Pardon our repetition, but it's so critical to understand this concept, and the other basic ones we've discussed, so that your advisor can be helpful in assuring that the life insurance proceeds remain outside of your estate.

Life insurance can also be used to replace assets that you donate during your lifetime, or upon your death, with the proceeds of life insurance that will remain outside of your estate. Since your heirs will lose any benefit from the donated property, you may use the tax deductions to purchase life insurance and make them the beneficiaries of the life insurance.

Let's talk a little bit more about Irrevocable Life Insurance Trusts (ILITs), which are a method of eliminating the ownership of an insurance policy from your estate while deriving all of the tax free benefits that apply to your beneficiaries. If drafted properly and funded appropriately, the proceeds of the policy will not be included in your estate and your heirs will receive a large sum of money (liquidity) with which to pay your estate tax liabilities. It will also replace the asset that is being donated to charity if you have created a Charitable Remainder Trust (CRT) and the heirs will not receive the property that is going to charity.

However, the trust and the method of payment must be strictly adhered to for this process to achieve these objectives. The life insurance policy will be owned by an irrevocable trust, which is a separate document from your living trust. The goal is for the proceeds to avoid taxation on your estate and to avoid probate, while providing your heirs with liquidity to quickly pay any of the estate tax liabilities.

Be forewarned, the trust is irrevocable; it cannot be modified once the assets have been transferred.

An attorney with experience in creating ILITs must draft the documents. Next, an insurance advisor with experience and expertise in estate planning and life insurance should be consulted. Once you have determined the amount of insurance that will be required—and this can only be an estimate, as property values and family members change— you will do one of two things: If you have an existing policy that is suitable, it may be transferred into the trust. If an existing policy is used, you must live for a minimum of three more years to avoid the estate tax. This is risky. An alternative is to have the trust purchase a new policy on your life under which you can pass away the next day with all of the tax benefits intact. Such an option is preferable if you are in good health and insurable, which leads us to the next step.

If the estate is structured properly, the tax burden will fall primarily on the estate of the last spouse to die. As a result of the unlimited marital deduction and the maximum use of exemptions, the bulk of your estate will go to your spouse and vice-versa. To reduce the cost of the life insurance and to provide the liquidity for the estate taxes, it makes sense to insure the last to die.

Assuming that both spouses are alive, most advisors will recommend that you purchase a whole life insurance policy on both spouses that will pay when the last spouse passes away. This is known as a "last to die" policy.

There is one more problem: Who should pay the premiums on the policy? The correct answer is critical to your estate planning and necessary to avoid further taxation. The heirs are the likely source for the payment of the premiums.

Why? Because your heirs will be the beneficiaries of your generosity. How, though, do they find the money to pay the premiums?

Most collectors should use the annual gift tax exemption to give their heirs an amount that will cover the cost of the premiums. Remember, you can make annual gifts of $14,000 or $28,000 if your spouse joins you. You are essentially purchasing a life insurance policy to benefit your heirs, while at the same time giving them cash gifts with which to pay the premiums. Life (insurance) is not always fair.

There is also another word of caution:

These gifts must be gifts of "present interest" to qualify for the annual gift tax exemption; ask your attorney. To qualify for the exclusion, you must give the heirs the right to reject the gift, usually for a period of 30 days. That creates a present gift. These gifts will be transferred to the trust where, as we discussed, the funds will be used to pay for the life insurance premiums. The factors that make this a present rather than future gift are known as the "Crummey powers." They are named after an astute, fabulously-named, and somewhat obsessive taxpayer who argued to the IRS that these annual gifts are gifts of present interest.

One last problem: There are many forms of life insurance. There are whole life policies, term policies, universal life, variable life policies and many, many more. Without going into a detailed study of life insurance, be forewarned: DO NOT, UNDER ANY CIRCUMSTANCES, USE TERM LIFE INSURANCE TO FUND THE TRUST. Use a form of whole life insurance. Term insurance may be cheaper, but it may expire before you do and will have no benefit in terms of funding the policy if it is no longer in effect when you pass away. It is a good idea, in certain circumstances, but not in funding an ILIT, and not for estate planning purposes.

Whole life insurance, whether variable or universal life, or other permanent insurance, should be used to assure that the funds will be available should you live to be 120 years old. Also, when term insurance expires, you may not be insurable and term insurance premiums increase exponentially after age 60. A whole life policy will cover the last to die. There may be exceptions to this rule, so speak with your advisor if term life is recommended for the ILIT.

In addition, the trust will have the ability to borrow from the cash value of a whole life policy for other needs without income tax consequences. Variable life policies actually allow the trustee to invest the cash value in a number of investments, such as mutual funds and bond funds (but not art or collectibles). These investments can be transferred within the policy from fund to fund without any tax consequences, which is an attractive benefit. However, should these investments go down, there may be additional cash required to maintain the policy benefits.

TIPS FOR HEIRS: An ILIT is an important planning tool that provides liquidity to pay for any estate tax liabilities; the proceeds are not included in your estate. You may gift the premium amounts to your heirs using the annual gift tax exclusion and the proceeds will be received tax free to your heirs to be used to pay the estate taxes and all's well that ends well. It is important that the documents are drafted properly by an expert and the gifts are made in accordance with IRS rulings. Insurance is a critical strategy for any substantial estate. Make an expert a part of your team.

Kathleen Guzman's Story ....

Kathleen Guzman is a managing director at Heritage Auctions, having joined the firm in 2006 after a career that included serving as President of Christie's East and President of Phillips Auctioneers, and as Senior Vice-President of Business Development at eBay. She has appeared as an antiques expert on Oprah, Good Morning America, Today, and CNN, and is probably best recognized for having served as an appraiser on Antiques Roadshow for more than 20 years.

Sometimes the business of treasure hunting and treasure-dealing has a way of imitating the stories behind the objects collectors covet. The best example of this phenomenon in my career came in 1994, when I orchestrated the sale of the original Maltese Falcon.

In the 1941 movie classic *The Maltese Falcon* — based on the 1931 Dashiell Hammett novel of the same name — Casper Gutman (played by Sydney Greenstreet) offers private investigator Sam Spade (Humphrey Bogart) $25,000 plus a quarter of the sale proceeds for help locating a figurine of a black bird believed to be filled with priceless jewels.

In 1994 — by which time the film was widely considered the first example of film noir and had recently been added to the Library of Congress' National Film Registry — I was the president of Christie's East, and a lady named Tippy Stringer called our Beverly Hills office about a few items she was looking to sell, so I headed out to have a look.

Stringer was one of the first female weather reporters and a television legend in her own right, but the marquee lot of her collection came from her late husband, the actor William Conrad. Sitting on the shelf in Stringer's library — in the background, propping up a row of leather-bound books — was the original Maltese Falcon used in the movie, a gift to Conrad from Warner Bros. studio head Jack Warner.

The Maltese Falcon, an elusive object in the movie, is an elusive object in real life — and the object I was looking at had been presumed lost for decades. The Warner Brothers Archives cite two examples produced for the film, which the stage hands remember using for weightlifting competitions; they weighed 45 pounds each, and one of them was in the collection of a California dentist. During the filming of the movie, the statue fell from actress Lee Patrick's hands — and landed on Bogart's left foot, causing a minor injury. Seeing it on the shelf, then taking it down to examine it and noticing the Warner Brothers prop house number, my hands trembled.

On December 6, 1994, the Maltese Falcon was up for auction — the highlight of the film and television memorabilia sale — and I was the auctioneer in a sale that also included Academy Awards for *Gone With the Wind* and a copy of that book signed by the cast of the movie.

The pre-sale estimate was $30,000-$50,000, but intense interest at the viewing and a few absentee bids had driven our internal estimate up to $150,000. Film noir buffs had traveled far to see the prop — some came dressed as Humphrey Bogart hoping to take a picture with it, and one lady came looking to measure it for the design of the table she was planning to build for it. That kind of interest is every seller's dream, but also created the potential for an unhappy experience for auction-goers. Our inadvertently low estimate had brought out more than a few people who thought they would have a shot at the falcon for a fraction of what we by then knew it would sell for.

I instantly knew what to do. I wanted to lighten the atmosphere in the room and give every auction-goer a chance to at least bid on it: so I started the bidding at one dollar. Every hand in the room shot up, and the place roared with laughter. The people there got the memory of their lives and they were able to tell their families and friends that they bid on the Maltese Falcon!

When the hammer came down, the Maltese Falcon Sold for: $398,500, a record price for a film prop at the time, and also surely a record price for a lead bird with a bronze patina! The buyer was Ronald Winston, president of the New York-based Harry Winston jewelry chain — but before he could be identified by the press gathered there, Winston fled the room. The newscasts that night showed the flight of the mysterious buyer of the Maltese Falcon. When Winston formally announced his acquisition, there were high hopes, based on the family's past generosity, that the piece would end up in the Smithsonian. But it was not meant to be: the Maltese Falcon was reportedly sold to a reclusive sheikh for more than a million dollars, and the elusive bird has not been seen since.

1952 Topps Mickey Mantle #311 PSA NM-MT 8.
Sold for: $501,900 | February 2016

8

Collectibles and Charitable Giving

"In faith and hope the world will disagree, But all mankind's concern is charity." – Alexander The Great

"To give requires good sense." – Ovid

A mericans gave $358 billion to charity in 2014, and individual donors contributed close to three-quarters of that amount; in total, charitable giving represents about 2% of GDP.

People are charitable for a variety of reasons. Many are motivated by pure altruism and others seek public acknowledgment. While you may not be charitable by nature, a charitable gift can be used in conjunction with other strategies to reduce or eliminate taxes. Tax laws provide benefits to those who donate in order to encourage greater donations. Charitable tax deductions share the cost of operating these institutions that provide essential functions.

Charitable Giving Nuts and Bolts

For tax purposes, a charitable gift makes the most sense when a collection has incurred substantial capital gains from appreciation. Property presently valued at less than its original cost should generally be sold at a loss rather than donated to charity.

This is because the amount of your deduction is based upon the fair market value of the property and not the original cost to you. If you give a gift to the appropriate charity, with a fair market value of $50,000 that originally cost $10,000, you will receive a deduction for the entire $50,000. This is the benefit of a charitable donation that has appreciated in value. When looking at the tax implications of a charitable gift, it is imperative that you involve your tax planner, attorney, and financial advisor, because the rules are complicated.

If your collection has appreciated, you may be able to enjoy some fiscal benefit through a charitable donation to a public charity. Here is what it takes to qualify:

1. The donated items are qualified capital gains property

This generally means that the donated items have been in the collection for at least a year, are not tangible items created by you (because if they were, you would only be allowed to deduct the cost of materials in most cases), and were not gifted to you by their creator.

2. The donee organization is a qualified public charity

Public charities generally receive at least part of their support from the public. IRS Section 501(c)(3) lists the types of donee organizations and the guidelines for them to follow to qualify for the charitable deduction. The charity must serve a public interest and must meet an "organizational test." Additionally, the organization must be organized and operated for a religious, charitable, scientific, literary, or educational purpose.

Churches, schools and museums are generally considered to be qualified public charities, while private foundations are not. The difference is that you receive a deduction based only upon the actual cost of the donated item when you give to a private foundation, while a public charitable donation can be deducted at full fair market value. It is reasonable for a potential donor to request that an organization write a letter confirming that the IRS has made a determination that the organization qualifies for tax-exempt status under Section 501(c)(3), and that the charity intends to use the objects for a valid charitable purpose.

3. The donee organization must make "related use" of the donation

Your gift of tangible personal property must relate to the exempt purposes or functions of the organization. For example, if you donate a coin collection to the American Numismatic Society for the purpose of expanding its museum collections, you would receive a deduction of fair market value since the collection relates to the Society's mission of increasing the knowledge and enjoyment of coin collecting.

If you donate that collection to a hospital that intends to sell the collection and use the revenue for its capital campaign, you can only deduct your cost of acquisition. The difference between types of use is subjective and often confusing, so it is important to determine the use for the gift. Make sure that the qualified organization actually wants the donation. The organization should provide a written acceptance of the collection or item, stating that it is a qualified public charity and that the donation satisfies the related use rule.

An additional factor, which reinforces the importance of communicating with the charity, is that a charitable deduction for contributions of tangible personal property exceeding $5,000 must be reduced or recaptured if the donee sells the property for less than your deducted amount within three years of the contribution.

4. The collection has a "qualified appraisal"

The IRS requires a qualified appraisal if the gift of property is more than $5,000. If the gift is greater than $20,000, a complete copy of the signed appraisal must be attached to the tax return.

A qualified appraisal is defined by the IRS; your advisor should be familiar with these requirements, and we discuss this in more depth later. A qualified appraiser is an individual who holds himself out to the public as an appraiser and has earned an appraisal designation from a recognized professional organization or has otherwise met certain education and experience requirements, regularly performs appraisals for compensation, and meets any other IRS requirements.

Other Issues in Charitable Giving

Most charities know very little about collectible assets. If you want your donation to be a meaningful contribution, you have to determine how the charity will use your collection.

In most cases, that means that it will have to sell your collection to raise funds. Unless you are donating the collection to a museum that will display it or use it for research, it is probably best to dispose of it in your lifetime while you are able to enjoy the good works that the donation can create. If you cannot tolerate the idea of selling your collection, then you should leave detailed written instructions for the disposition of your gift. As wonderful as charities are, they are likely to have less affection for your collection than an heir, and a greater interest in putting your donation to good use by converting it to cash.

In light of these concerns, an auction is a popular choice. It is imperative that you select an auctioneer with experience in your field. The charity of choice can be named as beneficiary of the proceeds from the auction. Assisting the charity in planning for the sale of your collection ensures that the charity will receive the maximum return without exhausting its own resources.

Limitations and the Five-Year Carryover

What if you donate an item of very large value that results in a very large tax deduction relative to your income level?

The IRS limits the amount of a charitable income tax deduction to a percentage of current income. If the donation is made to a qualified public charity, and the gift is considered a related use, you can deduct the current fair market value up to 30% of your adjusted gross income. If the donation is made to a qualified public charity, but is a non-related use, then your deduction is limited to your cost basis up to 50% of your adjusted gross income. However, you can carry forward the excess deductions for up to five years, until the amount is fully deducted.

For example, a collector with an adjusted gross income of $100,000 has a coin that he purchased for $50,000 in 1985; it is now worth $150,000. The collector donates it to a museum that plans to exhibit it. Because the donation is to a qualifying organization and is a related use, he can deduct the fair market value of $150,000, subject to a limit of 30% of his current adjusted gross income. Therefore, in the current year he is able to deduct $30,000 and can carry forward the remaining $120,000 in deductions over the next four years.

Donating a Fractional interest

Fractional giving is a process where you donate percentages of ownership of a collection or single object over a multi-year time frame. The percentage that you donate is the percentage that you can receive as a charitable tax deduction. Historically, it benefited public institutions while it allowed the donors both estate and capital gains tax deductions. It provided the added benefit of allowing the donor to retain possession for a period of time and the affiliation of the collection with the museum has the potential to increase the collection's value (and increase the charitable tax deduction).

The Pension Protection Act of 2006 directs donors to gift the entire interest in the collection to the charity within 10 years of the initial donation, or death, whichever comes first. Also, the donee institution must maintain substantial physical possession of the object within 10 years of the initial contribution. Since the laws involving fractional giving remain in a state of flux, fractional gifts may be a very difficult estate planning option. Collectors who are considering making fractional gifts should obtain expert advice prior to gifting.

Charitable Remainder Trusts

A charitable remainder trust (CRT) is beneficial if you want both income and a tax deduction, and are prepared to give up your collection now.

It is particularly advantageous if the collection has enjoyed significant appreciation since the time of acquisition, and you are no longer emotionally attached to it. In this arrangement, the donation is made to the qualifying charity in trust. The charity agrees to pay you annually, either a fixed amount of money (annuity trust) or a percentage of the trust's total value (unitrust) for life, or for a set number of years (not to exceed 20).

The benefit is that if you sold the collection yourself to create income, the principal amount would be reduced by the taxes on the capital gains (28%). In a CRT, the trustee can sell the collection tax free and create a larger principal base. You can claim the collection's future or remainder value (based on IRS tables) as a charitable deduction in the year that the property is transferred to the trust because the trust is considered a "non-related use." You receive your agreed-upon payments and when the trust period is complete, all remaining interest in the trust passes to the charity with both you and the institution avoiding capital gains taxes on the appreciated value of the items. Ultimately, you receive a regular income stream, while avoiding estate taxes and probate by transferring the asset out of the estate.

There are some caveats. Most collectibles are not "income producing assets," so the collection – at least most of it – may have to be sold within the first year of the trust in order to fund it with qualifying financial vehicles. The annual distribution to the donor must be a minimum of 5% of the trust's value and a maximum of 50%. Additionally, at the conclusion of the agreement, the remainder to the qualified charity must be at least 10% of the initial value. These rules are subject to change, and create a certain amount of latitude in the trust agreement that must be negotiated between the donor and the charity. Again, we strongly recommend that you use the services of a competent estate planning attorney or tax advisor.

A charitable remainder trust is a gift that keeps on giving. This may be one of the few gifts that you may ever receive from the IRS. Where else in the Internal Revenue Code are you able to make a charitable donation, receive an immediate tax deduction which may be carried forward if necessary, and reduce your estate and potential estate tax while you receive an income for a period of years without paying? You guessed it: The 28% capital gain on the appreciation of your collectibles.

Other Trust Variations

Trusts are complex legal documents that must be drafted properly or you may lose all of the potential tax benefits. An expert is required to avoid future distress. The trust is irrevocable and once property is transferred, only a few minor changes are permitted without harmful results. There are a number of variations on the charitable remainder trust known as CRATs, CRUTs, and GRUTs. At the time you transfer your collectibles to the trust, you will be entitled to an immediate income tax deduction. Retain a qualified appraiser who is familiar with the IRS rules, and an appraisal to support the value of the property.

The IRS, as we have and will discuss, has strict rules regarding the qualifications for a qualified appraiser and appraisal. The amount of the deduction is the fair market (not the actual cost) value of the assets discounted over the length of the trust assuming you have owned these objects for more than one year.

1913 5C Liberty PR64 NGC
The Olsen Specimen
Sold for: $3,737,500 | January 2010

The length of the trust may be term certain (not to exceed 10 years) or it may continue over the term of your life, or the lives of you and your spouse. The longer the term of the trust, the less the charitable deduction. For example, the trust distributions may endure for a maximum of 20 years, or for the rest of your life, or for the rest of yours and your spouse's life.

The amount of the immediate deduction may offset only 30% of your adjusted gross income in the first year; however, if the deduction cannot be fully used in the first year, it may be carried forward for up to five years. The trust is tax exempt and is able to sell appreciated assets without incurring any capital gains. This means that the full sale proceeds (not just the after-tax portion) can be invested to generate an annual income for life for you and/or your spouse.

Here is what this means. If you sold your collection today for $3 million, and you paid $1 million for it 10 years ago, you would likely pay the 28% capital gains tax, which would leave you with a $560,000 tax bill.

The net amount available for investment would be $2,440,000 ($3,000,000 less the $560,000 tax) that you could invest as you may determine. However, the trust will be able to invest the entire $3,000,000 and provide you with an income for life, or lives, or up to 20 years at a rate that the donor (you) determines with the charity. The asset is now out of your estate and no longer subject to estate taxes.

The only other rules are that the annual distributions from the trust must be a minimum of 5% of the value, and a maximum of 50%. Also, at the time the trust ends, the remainder that goes to the charity must be at least 10% of the initial value of the contribution.

This is the ideal solution for anyone whose collection has appreciated significantly in value who would like to sell the collection and does not have heirs interested in owning the collectibles.

The other, less favorable, alternative is to retain the collection until you die whereupon your heirs will receive a stepped-up basis if they sell the assets. The assets, though, will be included in the value of the estate, which may in itself create a tax if exemptions do not preclude estate taxation at the time of death.

Charitable Remainder Trust Example

The easiest and most understandable way to explain the charitable remainder trust concept is by way of example. We will use stocks, where the capital gains tax is currently 15%—which is much less than the maximum rate of 28% for collectibles. The theory is the same and you can understand the positive results:

- Martha Smith is 75 years old.
- She owns 500 shares of BP that are worth $100,000 today.
- The shares were purchased for $20,000 15 years ago.
- She does not want to pay the 15% capital gains tax.
- She establishes a CRAT, charitable remainder annuity trust. She transfers the stock into the trust.
- The CRAT sells the stock and invests the proceeds into bonds or dividend-paying stocks.
- The CRAT pays no tax on the capital gain when the assets are sold.
- The CRAT pays Martha 10% of the net fair market value of the trust annually for the rest of her life. The return may be negotiated subject to guidelines.
- The CRAT pays Martha $10,000 in the first year—10% of $100,000. She will receive this amount every year until she dies. If she has a spouse, it would continue for both of their lives or a set period up to 10 years from the date of transfer of the assets.
- Martha receives an immediate tax deduction of $41,119.
- Martha uses her large deduction to purchase a life insurance policy to transfer into her ILIT with her heirs as beneficiaries.

- Martha will gift enough money to her heirs each year using her annual exclusion of $14,000 to pay the insurance premiums.
- The heirs will pay the amount to the trust that is needed for the life insurance premiums.
- The $100,000 of BP is no longer in Martha's estate.
- When Martha dies, her heirs will receive the proceeds from the life insurance, tax-free.

In essence, Martha will not have to pay any of the capital gains tax on the appreciation of the assets, she will have an immediate tax deduction of $41,119, she will receive $10,000 per year for her life and the stock is no longer part of her estate subject to the estate tax. In fact, she has basically eliminated or diminished both potential estate and capital gains taxes. If she had a spouse, she and her spouse could choose to receive income for the rest of both of their lives.

There is also a vehicle known as a NIMCRUT, which is a variation of a CRT that will allow the trust to make up in future years distributions that it could not pay from earnings on the investments of the trust. If the trust has agreed to pay 6% per year to the donor, or donors, and there is not sufficient income from the investments to pay the full amount, it has the ability to make up the difference to the donor by the time the trust terminates. These funds could be used for retirement purposes as part of your retirement plan.

TIPS FOR HEIRS: In summary, when it comes to charitable planning and your collection, there are many options available to you, each with benefits and pitfalls. However, the laws are so complex in the area of charitable giving that even the most seasoned tax professional may not understand the full implications of a charitable gift. When considering making a charitable gift, it is extremely important that you collaborate with your advisory team and the charitable institution to ensure that your gift will provide both you and the organization with the maximum benefits.

Maxfield Parrish (American, 1870-1966)
Jason and His Teacher, Collier's magazine frontispiece and
A Wonder Book and *Tanglewood Tales* interior illustration, 1909
Oil on canvas laid on board
40 x 32 inches
Sold for : $1,025,000 | November 2015

PART THREE

Evaluating Your Collection

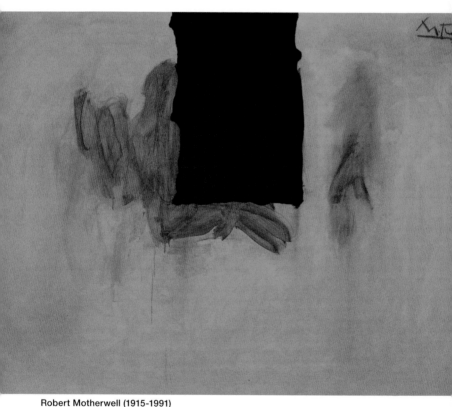

Robert Motherwell (1915-1991)
Untitled (Ochre with Black Line), 1972-73/1974
Acrylic and charcoal on canvas
55-3/4 x 74 inches
Sold for: $965,000 | October 2015

:
:
:
:
:

9

Third-Party Authentication and Grading

Authenticity and evaluation are vital matters for any collection. This chapter concentrates on third-party grading services that are available to grade and authenticate your collectibles. These services are widely available for coins, sports cards and comics. Use them as needed, but consider the cost, quality and value of grading services for your collectibles. For many items, especially lesser-valued pieces, grading may not be necessary.

For coin grading, the American Numismatic Association (ANA) adopted Dr. William Sheldon's 70-point grading system and, between 1973 and 1977, worked to establish standards for all series under the leadership of numismatic luminary Abe Kosoff. Experts from all coin specialties collaborated with Kosoff to develop the first official ANA grading guide, published in 1978.

Initially, it recognized three grades to evaluate Mint State coins: Uncirculated or MS-60; Choice Uncirculated or MS-65; and Perfect Uncirculated or MS-70. Unfortunately, the third grade (MS-70) was mostly theoretical, and the two remaining designations quickly proved inadequate for the marketplace. MS-63 (Select Uncirculated) and MS-67 (Gem Uncirculated) were added to the system and functioned successfully for a while until the demand for closer evaluation required additional grades. Eventually, all numbers between MS-60 and MS-70 were employed and the adjectival equivalents were eliminated.

NGC and PCGS remain the acknowledged leaders for coin grading. The reason for their success is that they are the only firms that have maintained sufficient dealer confidence to allow coins to be traded routinely on a sight-unseen basis.

Comics and cards are generally graded on a 10-point scale, with a "10" being the highest grade (most perfect quality). Several grading services are listed for these collectible categories in the Appendix. For comics, Comics Guaranty, LLC (CGC) is recognized as the most trusted grading service. Heritage Comics (comics.HA.com) offers a discount on standard CGC grading costs.

Sports card authenticity is often entrusted to one of three major grading houses: Professional Sports Authenticator (PSA), Beckett Grading Services (BGS) and Sportscard Guaranty LLC (SGC). Talk to your local card dealers, or find one online, and ask which grading service has the most credibility among dealers and collectors. Collectors' autographed items use PSA/DNA to authenticate their collectibles. They, too, are listed in the Appendix to this book.

Stamp collectors frequently rely on the grading services of Professional Stamp Experts (PSE). The PSE Web site (see Appendix) contains detailed instructions and an online submission kit, both of which are excellent guides on how to properly submit stamps for grading.

What Should You Certify?

Certification is an expensive proposition that should be approached with caution. At $15-$85 an item, the total costs, for even a small collection, can easily run into the thousands of dollars. Not all collectibles benefit equally from being certified. The rule of thumb, of course, is that the finished product has to be worth more than the raw (ungraded) item, plus the certification fee.

There are two practical reasons to certify a collectible: To determine authenticity and to add value.

When a dealer considers buying an uncertified collectible, he is trying to guess how the grading service is going to grade it—and he'll want to be as conservative as possible. For example, if a dealer is looking at your 1886-O Morgan dollar and he is trying to decide whether NGC will grade it an MS-63 (valued at, say, $3,000) or MS-64 (valued at $10,000), he will designate it as an MS-63 coin to be on the safe side, and offer a price commensurate with an MS-63 coin.

"La Madona Rosa"
Lavra Berilo Branco, Sapucaia do Norte, Galiléia,
Doce Valley, Minas Gerais, Brazil
Sold for: $662,500 | June 2013

You could, however, have the coin certified before attempting to sell it. Your upside is that if the grading service calls it an MS-64, you have a five-figure coin. The downside is the cost of the grading fee. The bottom line is that this issue has a significant value spread between grades and—in our opinion—the risk is worth the expense.

Submitting Your Coins

NGC and PCGS both operate primarily through authorized dealer networks, though both offer programs where collectors can directly submit coins to the grading services. Most of these dealers will frequently submit your coins to the grading services on your behalf. The dealer is often compensated with a rebate of approximately 20% of the grading fee. Don't request part of the rebate, but do ask him or her to preview the coins and help you determine which coins to submit for certification. Most authorized dealers are familiar with the standards of both grading services and can help you avoid submitting coins where third-party grading may not add value.

If you reside within driving distance of an authorized dealer, make an appointment to preview the coins with them. If you are not within a reasonable distance, you may ship your coins to an authorized dealer of your choice. A good rule of thumb is to select an authorized dealer who is also a member of the Professional Numismatists Guild (PNG). The PNG is the most respected numismatic fraternal organization and each new candidate must undergo a detailed background check and be approved by the entire membership. Members must conduct themselves under a strict Code of Ethics and submit to binding arbitration in the event of disputes. Contact information for the PNG is also included in the Appendix A.

Declaring Submission Value for Insurance

When you prepare to submit your collectibles for grading, you will be asked to declare a value for insurance purposes. This is important should the package become lost or the items damaged in transit or at the grading service. Since grading and shipping fees are both impacted by this decision, you need to determine whether the value range is commensurate with the likelihood of loss or damage, and then select a replacement value for the items. Third-party grading can be an extremely important part of estate planning. Certification by a reputable grading system will increase the liquidity of your collection when it is sold because certified coins are easy to trade among dealers, and on the Internet. Your heirs and advisors will be spared the burden of extensive (and expensive) identification and cataloging.

Third-party grading will protect your collectibles, allow your heirs to value and identify them, and provide liquidity when the collection is sold.

TIPS FOR HEIRS: As a non-collector, submitting items for third-party grading and authentication for the important items in your inheritance will provide you and your heirs with a far greater comfort level in assessing the real value of the collection. Because you are probably unfamiliar with the language and nuances of the hobby, we recommend that you devote additional time to qualifying the authorized dealer you consult. Speak plainly about your goals and ask a lot of questions. If you are not satisfied with the responses to your questions, don't hesitate to request a more detailed explanation. You can never know too much about your inheritance, but knowing too little can be extremely dangerous.

Fakes in the Market at all Values ·········

As those who counterfeit goods become more sophisticated, so must the techniques used to detect them. An auction house or dealer should actively seek to authenticate your items and reach out to the leading experts to verify an object's authenticity.

For paintings, it may be the individual, committee or foundation that has published the catalogue raisonné of the artist's works. Coins, stamps, sports cards, comics and other collectibles each have leading third-party grading and authentication services that certify items.

Yet, despite the best due diligence, fakes can infiltrate all levels of the market, from top to bottom.

In coins there are contemporary counterfeit Morgan silver dollars that have only recently have been revealed by sharp-eyed scholars. Contemporary counterfeits are pieces that were produced and circulated around the time of genuine issues. They are not to be confused with modern fakes and today, known contemporary counterfeits are widely collected. In May 2016 a new counterfeit 1894-O Morgan dollar was discovered. Likely produced between 1902 and 1904, that this variety was revealed as a contemporary counterfeit has little impact on its market value.

Today more deceptive fakes in nearly all collectible categories are being made in China, by craftsmen and women who take great pride in their ability to copy luxury brands, rare coins, wine and nearly everything else of value.

For most objects, a branding of being fake can destroy the value. Fakes were at the center of the sudden demise of New York's venerable Knoedler & Co. gallery in 2011. The gallery had enjoyed continuous operation since 1846, but a scandal involving a group of Abstract Expressionist fakes of works purportedly by Jackson Pollock, Mark Rothko and others, led to lawsuits which forced its closure.

The paintings were sold by the gallery between 1994 and 2011, purchased from a Long Island art dealer who had obtained the paintings from a Chinese art forger who allegedly painted the pictures in his Queens garage and sold them for less than $9,000 each. In 2013 the Long Island dealer pleaded guilty to selling over 60 fake works of art.

The subsequent lawsuits included many of the world's top collectors including Italian fashion and auction house executive Domenico De

A Group of Five Dossiers ff Photographs and Documentation of Fake Renoir Works
Sold for: $3,750 | Sept 2013

Sole, who sued the gallery and its former president Ann Freedman for $25 million after purchasing a fake Rothko picture from the gallery for $8.3 million.

The trial, which kicked off on Jan. 25, 2016, was ended two weeks later when Freeman and the gallery settled with De Sole and his wife. After the settlement, De Sole said, "My point of view was, 'Fine, if it's authentic, give me my $8.3 million back and I'll walk away. Now you can sell this authentic Rothko for more than twice as much, $18 million, or whatever and you can make a huge profit.' When they absolutely refused to do that I knew that, one, the Rothko was definitely a fake, and two, they knew for sure that it was a fake."

As fakes become better, so must a collector's sophistication in detecting them. Artists have long been concerned with how fakes might tarnish their legacy. French Impressionist Pierre-Auguste Renoir was concerned with both fakes of his works and the addition of fake signatures to his works. On Sept. 13, 2013, Heritage sold the single largest archive of Renoir's personally-owned objects. Among these was a single lot consisting of five notebooks of authentication requests from around the world, as well as his son Claude "Coco" Renoir's attestations and other correspondence concerning authenticity issues, supplemented by photographs and additional related material. It Sold for: $3,750 – and was most assuredly authentic!

1965 Muhammad Ali & Sonny Liston Fight Worn
Gloves-Both Pairs from the Famous "Phantom
Punch" Bout.
Sold for: $956,000 | February 2015

10

Having Your Collection Appraised

The appraisal of collectibles and other tangible personal property is an integral part of estate planning. Appraisals are required for estate tax, charitable contributions and gift tax purposes as well as for divorce settlements, and many insurance policies.

A key element in the process is the selection of an appraiser. In rare coins, for instance, the appraiser must be familiar with trends in the entire rare coin market as well as the individual specialization areas they may have in order to provide accurate appraisals that can be submitted to the IRS.

U.S. rare coins have independent pricing guides that are published weekly, along with recognized, independent certification services and a strong established auction history. However, some rare coins are rather esoteric and require a skilled appraiser to evaluate the factors of provenance, rarity, variety, type, quality and, where uncertified coins are involved, the condition based on contemporary standards.

Appraising art and paper collectibles (rare books, comics, and art) often requires an appraiser with a trained eye for the works of particular artists and a comprehensive understanding of the current market for those particular genres of the collectibles. It may be necessary to speak with several appraisers before choosing one with the particular expertise that is required. Heritage Auctions Appraisal Services (HA.com/Appraise) can assist you with finding a qualified appraiser either from our in-house experts or from our network of ethical professionals.

IRS regulation 170(f)(11)(E)(ii) provides that the term "qualified appraiser" is defined as an individual, who (1) has earned an appraisal designation from a recognized professional appraiser organization, or has otherwise met minimum education and experience requirements set forth in regulations prescribed by the Secretary, (2) regularly performs appraisals for which the individual receives compensation, and (3) meets other such requirements as may be prescribed by the Secretary in regulations or other guidance.

It is also important that the appraiser is aware of the IRS rules governing appraisals. Neither the IRS nor Congress has yet sought to unify the appraisal requirements for income tax, estate tax or gift tax pur- poses. Crucial differences exist, such as (1) the requirement that certain estate tax, but not income tax or gift tax appraisals, be made under oath, and (2) the minimum values (e.g. $5,000 and $50,000), above which special appraisal requirements apply. Therefore, when obtaining an appraisal for tax purposes, you should be careful to clearly explain the specific tax purpose to your appraiser and review the completed appraisal.

Each party involved in the appraisal process may have different motivations that would favor a higher or lower value for a given object. For gifts and estate tax purposes, lower appraised valuations are likely preferred by the taxpayer since lower values equal a lower tax burden. However, for transfers to a charitable trust, a higher valuation may increase the deduction and benefit the taxpayer. Higher valuations may affect the limitations imposed upon annual gift tax rules on the lifetime gift tax exemptions. The IRS may contend otherwise, should a dispute arise; so the appraisal must be able to withstand close scrutiny, which is one of the reasons an appraiser is subject to certain penalties in respect to the fairness and accuracy of the appraisal.

The Antiques Roadshow Factor

For professionals in the appraisal business, the subtitle of this section might be "How *Antiques Roadshow* Confuses Everyone."

We love *Antiques Roadshow*, of course, and as auctioneers serving collectors with many of Heritage's own experts on the show, we are very grateful for all the *Roadshow* has done to raise public awareness about— and enthusiasm for—collecting. By necessity, though, the show oversimplifies: fast, verbal descriptions of inconsistent value types, with all of the effort and intensive research edited out, appearing to flow extemporaneously from the mouths of apparently brilliant television personalities, all protected by the "entertainment-only" waiver protection that such shows enjoy.

One participant is told a value "in my retail shop," and another is told "at auction the estimate would be," and yet others are told "you might take home 'x' amount of dollars" for this item. Many different definitions of value are expressed without any basis or explanation for their differences and viewers at home are left with the presumption that all appraisals can be successfully completed in 20-second sound bites.

Finally, there is the "I-saw-one-just-like-it-on-*Antiques-Roadshow*" effect, encountered by professional appraisers everywhere, who are forced to explain why and how their client's item is not the same or similar to the one he saw on television. A formal "qualified appraisal" is a much more serious matter, with wide-ranging financial and legal repercussions.

The verbal appraisal is unacceptable for most business and all tax-related contexts. Video-taped inventories of your household property and quick "laundry list" appraisals do not fulfill the definition of a "qualified appraisal". Nor is a dealer's offered price to purchase your collection, or the estimates of an auction house.

The dealer's proposed price is not acceptable as a valid appraisal because the dealer has a financial interest in the property that they may be trying to acquire from you. Auction house estimates may—under certain, but not all circumstances—represent a qualified appraised value. Someone who must liquidate property at auction at any price to raise cash may reasonably agree and desire lower estimates in order to attract more spirited bidding. Auction prices may also be subject to rigged bidding or to overpricing when there are two or more bidders who are willing to pay any price to have the winning bid. As a result, auction prices and estimates are only one of several components of an appraisal that affects the valuation.

Adding to the confusion is the fact that any antique or collectible actually has several different values, the three most relevant being insurance value, fair market value, and marketable cash value. The

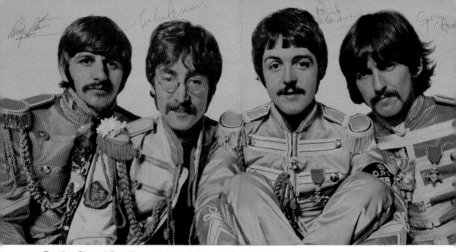

**Beatles Signed Sgt. Pepper's Lonely Hearts Club Band
Mono UK Gatefold Cover (Parlophone PMC 7027, 1967).**
Sold for: $290,500 | March 2013

purpose of an appraisal generally dictates which of these different value definitions is relevant.

An expert, detailed analysis with supporting data will allow you to defend the valuation designated by the appraisal should it become necessary. It is important to note that the IRS will assume a position, in any dispute, that is most favorable to them and not to you. Reasonable people may disagree and, most importantly, remember than any appraisal is as much an art as a science. There are many shades of grey between the black and white areas. However, keep in mind the general definition of value is the price that a willing buyer and a willing seller will negotiate with one another, with neither party under any compulsion to buy or sell.

An expert, detailed analysis with supporting data will allow you to defend the valuation designated by the appraisal should it become necessary. In the event of a dispute the IRS typically assumes positions most favorable to them and not the taxpayer. Reasonable people may disagree and, most importantly, remember than an appraisal is as much an art as a science.

Appraisal Regulations

There is no single, unified government document or regulation that comprehensively prescribes the appraisal content and processes required for income tax, estate tax, and gift tax purposes. A growing body of government, government-sponsored, and private organizations are more or less coordinating their efforts to regulate the appraisal industry and establish unified standards.

The Uniform Standards for Professional Appraisal Practice (USPAP), is published by the Appraisal Foundation, which is authorized by Congress as the source of appraisal standards and appraisal qualifications.

The Pension Protection Act of 2006 and its subsequent guidance radically changed the appraisal profession by legislating higher standards and increasing appraiser penalties.

The IRS has an assortment of regulatory requirements that are, scattered throughout the tax code. In practice, guidelines technically written for donation appraisals are often used as guidance for estate appraisals, and vice versa. This is despite the fact that the taxpayer will hope for a higher appraised value when making a charitable donation or transfer to a charitable trust and a lower valuation for estate tax purposes.

Each of the three major personal property appraisal organizations – the International Society of Appraisers, the Appraisers Association of America and the American Society of Appraisers - has its own written regulations, which members must follow. These standards are in tandem with the requirements set forth in USPAP.

A museum cataloging system known as the Getty Object ID is considered the standard for describing objects in a qualified appraisal, though the IRS has set preferences of how it would like items described in certain high value appraisals, along with preferred methods of imaging to be included with appraisals.

The wise appraiser uses a cumulative approach to the various regulatory requirements of each of these authorities in order to prepare a competent appraisal report that meets the client's expectations and fulfills the appraisal's intended use and users.

The most common situations in which tangible personal property must be valued for tax purposes when:

- A taxpayer claims a charitable deduction on his or her income tax return.
- An executor values a decedent's personal effects.
- A taxpayer reports the value of a gift on a gift tax return.

Other purposes are discussed in this text, including regulations governing excess benefit transactions that involve certain exempt organizations. In each case the taxpayer or executor may be required to supply or rely upon an appraisal of the property; and the specific requirements are different in each situation.

Different Types of Values and Appraisals

To understand the three most relevant definitions of value, we will use an example of an item that is brought to auction and is sold for a hammer price of $1,000. There is a 20% buyer's premium, $200, added to the cost of $1,000. The purchaser, who is a dealer, tries to sell the item in his store for $2,400. Since the buyer has to pay the premium of $200, his or her cost is the fair market value of $1,200. The marketable cash value is $800 which represents the actual sale or "hammer" price of the item less the seller's fee (20% in this example). The insurance value is $2,400 which is the retail sales price.

Income Tax and Charitable Donations

Charitable donation appraisals use Fair Market Value (FMV) as the controlling definition of value, and the appraisal report is essentially the same as for the estate tax appraisal. The IRS defines FMV as the price that property would sell for on the open market. It is the price that would be agreed on between a willing buyer and a willing seller, with neither being required to act, and both having reasonable knowledge of the relevant facts.

The most complex appraisal requirements are those required of a taxpayer claiming a charitable deduction. For any item of tangible personal property valued at more than $5,000, the taxpayer must obtain a "Qualified Appraisal" and attach an "Appraisal Summary" to the income tax return. If any item is valued at more than $50,000, the taxpayer must attach the Qualified Appraisal itself to the tax return rather than only the Summary Appraisal. The appraisal regulations under Section 170 specify in detail the requirements of a Qualified Appraisal. These requirements are also summarized in IRS Publication 561, "Determining the Value of Donated Property".

Taxpayers and advisors should keep in mind that this publication is intended only for assistance in preparing income tax returns, and is not applicable for estate or gift tax purposes, although many of the concepts are the same or similar.

The four general requirements of a Qualified Appraisal are:

A. It must be made not more than 60 days before the date of the contribution of the property to the charity and not later than the due date of the return on which a deduction for the contribution is claimed.

B. No part of the fee for the appraisal can be based on a percentage of the appraised value of the property.

C. It must be prepared and signed by a "Qualified Appraiser" and all appraisers who contribute to its preparation must also sign it.

D. It must include:

1. A detailed description of the property in a form that someone who is not generally familiar with the type of property would be able to recognize this particular item. For certified coins the description should include the certifying organization, such as PCGS, NGC or ANACS and the certification number on the case;

2. A description of the physical condition of the property. For certified coins the grade of the coin on the case is sufficient;

3. The date (or expected date) of contribution;

4. The terms of any agreement that the donor has entered into or expects to enter with regard to the property;

5. The name, address, and taxpayer ID number of the Qualified Appraiser or Appraisers and if the Qualified Appraiser is employed or engaged as an independent contractor by

another person or firm, the name, address and taxpayer ID number of that person or firm;

6. The qualifications of the Qualified Appraiser who signs the appraisal, including the appraiser's background, experience, education and any membership in professional appraisal associations;

7. A statement that the appraisal was prepared for income tax purposes;

8. The date or dates the property was valued;

9. The appraised fair market value on the date of the contribution;

10. The method of valuation used to determine the fair market value;

11. The specific basis for the valuation; and

12. A description of the fee arrangement between the donor and appraiser.

The regulations under Section 170 provide very detailed guidelines concerning the qualifications of a Qualified Appraiser. These guidelines are intended to ensure that the Qualified Appraiser is competent to make the appraisal and is sufficiently disinterested to be able to render an honest opinion of value. The regulations provide:

A. Certain individuals are not allowed to be Qualified Appraisers, including:

1. The donor of the property (or taxpayer who claims the deduction);

2. The recipient of the property;

3. A party to the transaction in which the donor acquired the property, such as the person who sold the property to the donor, unless the donor makes the donation within two months of acquiring the property and claims an appraised value no higher than the price at which it was acquired;

4. A person who regularly prepares appraisals for one of the above and who does not perform a majority of his or her appraisals for other persons;

Willem de Kooning (1904-1997)
East Hampton II, 1968
Oil on paper laid on canvas
41-3/4 x 30 inches
Sold for: $802,000 | May 2016

5. Or a person employed by or related to any of the above persons in (1), (2) or (3) above.

B. A Qualified Appraiser must certify on the Appraisal Summary that he or she:

1. Holds himself or herself out to the public as an appraiser, or performs appraisals on a regular basis;

2. Is qualified to make appraisals of the type of property being valued because of the qualifications in the appraisal;

3. Is not one of the excluded individuals named above;

4. Is not receiving an appraisal fee based upon a percentage of the appraised property value; and

5. Understands that there is a penalty for aiding and abetting tax fraud, up to and including a stint at Club Fed.

C. A person cannot be a Qualified Appraiser if the donor has knowledge of facts that would cause a reasonable person to expect that the appraiser will overstate the value of the donated property.

A taxpayer who claims a charitable deduction greater than $500 must attach IRS Form 8283 to their income tax return and complete Section A of the form, which requires detailed information about the donated property and the donation. When a taxpayer claims a deduction for an item valued at more than $5,000, he or she must also complete Section B of the form. Section B is the "Appraisal Summary."

The Appraisal Summary requires additional information about the donated property as well as the signature of the donee and a certification signed by the Qualified Appraiser containing the representations described above.

In 1996, the IRS issued Revenue Procedure 96-15, which provides the procedures through which a taxpayer may request from the IRS a binding (on the IRS and the taxpayer) "Statement of Value" as to any item of art that has been appraised at $50,000 or more. The taxpayer may then use the Statement of Value to substantiate the value of the property for income, estate or gift tax purposes.

Estate Tax Purposes

Unlike insurance appraisals which use replacement value, the type of value required for estate appraisals is Fair Market Value (FMV), a government-defined value construct that is found in approximately 250 different places in the tax code. While the IRS accepts the sale price of liquidated estate assets as the most probative evidence of the property's FMV, unsold estate assets must be appraised according to the FMV definition.

The FMV for estate purposes must be determined effective as of the date of death or, if so elected by the executor, an alternate legal (as opposed to actual) date of death six months later. FMV does not take into consideration possible future values. This fixed date of effect can be significant in today's fast rising art and collectibles market. Valuation as of the date of death and six months later may vary and affect the tax consequences on the estate. Obviously, you will want to elect the date that provides the lower of the two values to minimize your estate value.

For unsold estate property, appraisers typically determine FMV by applying a market comparison approach. Past sales results of similar items, in a typical marketplace, and within a timely period, are analyzed to determine the value of the estate item.

For items valued at or above $5,000, appraisal standards require that the appraiser list the comparables that have been used in arriving at a value. The sale venue, date, and location of the comparable's sale should be mentioned, as well as lot numbers and sale numbers in the case of public auctions. As the sale prices of the comparables used may not correspond to that of the determined value of the estate item, a detailed explanation of the relevance of these comparables is also required. Other factors affecting value—such as exhibition history, provenance, and condition—should also be documented. Tax court judges have rejected appraisals in the past, not for their opinions of value per se, but for failing to explain the reasoning behind them.

For items valued at $20,000 or more, the IRS requires the appraisal report include a good diagnostic photograph of the item. Artworks of this value and higher are also reviewed by the IRS Art Advisory

Panel, a committee of art experts from various fields, formed to police underreported valuations.

In a June 2016 article in Barron's, writer Karen Hube reports that currently "the Internal Revenue Service is rigorously scrutinizing appraisals of artworks above $50,000 and often demanding value adjustments that trigger unexpected and large tax bills, with penalties and interest added on." She sites the case of the estate of art collector Bernice Newberger whose Picasso painting was appraised for $5 million as of the date of her death in mid-2009 – but when it came to sale through auction later that same year, it fetched a staggering price of $12.9 million. "Four years later, in 2013, the IRS revised the date-of-death value to $10 million, noting that postmortem sales should be factored into appraisals. An unexpected $5 million was subject to the 40% estate tax and 20% in penalties."

"From 2011 to 2014, the IRS raised appraisals for estate- and gift-tax returns and lowered those for charitable deductions—both moves resulting in higher tax burdens—on 41% of the total 1,394 appraisals that it reviewed. In 2014, 58 out of the 159 estate appraisals the IRS panel scrutinized were increased from a total of $36.3 million to $66.8 million, an eye-watering 84%," reports Hube.

The article concludes with some practical advice: "So what's a collector to do? Estates should get two artwork appraisals. Heirs, in turn, should brace themselves for an IRS valuation audit and have a fallback plan for paying unexpected taxes, should the ruling go against them."

Collectors of high value works of art can also petition the IRS Art Advisory Panel for a statement of value prior to any filings, though if the IRS continues to consider market values after the date of death for an estate or the date of a charitable donation – even their own valuations could possibly be later amended.

There are also instances when the value of property might go down from the date of death.

When an estate includes household and personal effects, the executor must file and complete Schedule F of the estate tax return, itemizing the property and reporting its value. All items of property must be listed separately, except those with a value of less than $100. Items having a value less than $100, and contained in the same room on the date of death, can be grouped together. As an alternative to itemizing, the executor may provide a written statement, prepared under penalties of perjury, setting forth the aggregate value of the property as appraised by competent appraisers of recognized standing and ability (or by dealers in the class of property involved).

As a practical matter, in large estates one or more appraisers value almost all "miscellaneous property." The reasons for this include:

1. That the alternative to itemizing, mentioned above, requires that executors rely on appraisals by either a competent appraiser or a dealer, and

2. That the Internal Revenue Code prescribes penalties for both undervaluing and overvaluing estate property.

These penalties may be waived on a showing of "reasonable cause and good faith," which may be demonstrated by justifiable reliance on a professional appraisal. In determining whether reliance on a particular appraisal demonstrated "reasonable cause and good faith," the IRS will take into account:

1. The methodology and assumptions underlying the appraisal,

2. The appraised value,

3. The relationship between appraised value and purchase price,

4. The circumstances under which the appraisal was obtained, and

5. The appraiser's relationship to the taxpayer or to the activity in which the property is used.

Certain types of tangible personal property must be appraised separately; specifically, items having been marked artistic or intrinsic value in excess of $3,000, such as jewelry, furs, silverware, paintings, etchings, antiques, books, vases, oriental rugs or coin and stamp collections require separate appraisals. The appraisal of such items must be made by an "expert or experts," and it must be made under oath, an often overlooked requirement. The appraisal must also be accompanied by the executor's written statement, made under penalties of perjury, as to the completeness of the itemized list of such property and as to the disinterested character and the qualifications of the appraiser or appraisers.

The regulations provide little guidance regarding the preparation of estate tax appraisals. They merely provide guidance for appraisals of specific types of property:

1. Books in sets by standard authors should be listed in separate groups;

2. In listing paintings having artistic value, the size, subject, and artist's name should be stated;

3. In the case of oriental rugs, the size, make, and general condition should be given; and

4. In the case of silverware, sets of silverware should be listed in separate groups, groups of individual pieces of silverware should be weighed and the weights given in troy ounces and, in arriving at the value of silverware, the appraisers should take into consideration its antiquity, utility, desirability, condition and obsolescence.

Additional general and specific guidance for estate tax appraisals has been provided in Revenue Procedure 66-49, which suggests that, for general purposes, an appraisal report should contain at least the following:

1. A summary of the appraiser's qualifications;

2. A statement of value and the appraiser's definition of the value they obtained;

3. The basis upon which the appraisal was made;

4. The signature of the appraiser and the date the appraisal was made.

Gift Tax Purposes

A taxpayer who makes a completed gift is required to file a gift tax return on IRS Form 709 and, except to the extent of a deduction such as the charitable or marital deduction, pay tax on the transfer at graduated rates based on the value of the gift if the gift generates a tax in excess of the unified credit amount.

As addressed earlier in this book, as of 2016 annual gifts that are within the allowable amount of $14,000 per donor, or $28,000 if both spous- es, do not require the filing of a form or the payment of any tax. However, when the gifts exceed the annual limits and reduce the lifetime gift tax exemptions, a form must be completed to assist the IRS in the determination of the amount remaining in your exemption, as well as that of your spouse if joint gifts have been made or are contemplated.

The instructions for the gift tax return and the applicable regulations require that the taxpayer attach to the return either a detailed description of the method used to determine the fair market value of the gifted property or an appraisal of the gifted property.

The regulations provide specific guidance regarding the preparation of gift tax appraisals. Although fairly general and applicable to gifts of many types of property, the regulations specify that a gift tax appraisal contain the following information:

1. The date of the gift;
2. The date on which the gifted property was appraised and the purpose of the appraisal;
3. A description of the gifted property;
4. A description of the qualifications of the appraiser;
5. A description of the appraisal process used;
6. Any information considered in determining the appraised value;
7. The appraisal procedures followed, and the reasoning that supports the analyses, opinion and conclusions reached in the appraisal;
8. The valuation method used, the rationale for the valuation method, and the procedure used in determining the fair market value of the gifted property;

9. The specific basis for the valuation, such as specific comparable sales or transactions.

The regulations also specify that an individual must meet the following criteria to prepare a gift tax appraisal:

1. Holds himself or herself out to the public as an appraiser, or performs appraisals on a regular basis;

2. Is qualified to make appraisals of the type of property being valued because of their qualifications, as described in the appraisal; and

3. Is not the donor or recipient of the property or member of the family of the donor or recipient (which includes spouses, ancestors, lineal descendants and spouses of lineal descendants) or any person employed by the donor, the recipient, or a member of the family of either the donor or the recipient.

The rules for the appraisal of tangible personal property may seem complicated but can become critically important if the advisor engages an appraiser who is not thoroughly familiar with them. For this reason, an advisor should ensure that the appraiser has up-to-date knowledge of appraisal formats as well as the marketplace in which the most sustainable comparable values can be found.

Insurance Appraisal

Insurance value is also known as Retail Replacement Value (RRV). The intent is to provide a professionally determined basis for making an insured client financially whole in the event of theft, loss or damage as defined by the terms of the insurance policy of the client. It represents a premium value due based on the time involved in locating a replacement in a retail setting, without the element of finding a replacement in an alternate setting, or waiting for the best available replacement.

RRV is generally the highest definition of value taking into account that replacing an item may require such expenses as airfare to a specific destination, a large crating and freight bill and any number of related expenses.

Some insurance companies "cash out" only at the actual value needed to replace the item. For this reason it is important to determine an accurate and realistic insurance value rather than one that is unreasonably high. In certain situations, overpaying on premiums based upon an over-insured amount will not have any advantage. Depending on the language of your policy, an insurance company may exercise the option to replace the item with another one with similar qualities rather than "cashing out." We know of one dealer who was approached by a collector who had a collection of Hummel figurines insured at $100,000 based on prices in a book from the 1990s. The dealer's advice to the hapless collector? Pack the collection into your car, park it in an unsafe neighborhood, and leave the doors unlocked.

It is extremely important that an insurance appraisal report describe the item comprehensively and exhaustively so that an inferior example will not be provided as a replacement. Any extant restoration reports must be attached. Documented distinguishing features, and restoration history also facilitate identification, should the insured item be stolen.

Insurance appraisals may require that the location of the item be noted, and any adverse factors related to it be included. Photographs are typically required for insurance appraisals.

You should insure your collection whether you maintain it in a safe-deposit box or at home, and particularly if you exhibit or trade portions of it at shows. Your insurance company will probably require an appraisal prior to granting coverage, but even if it is not required, it is in your best interests to secure one. The premiums will be assessed on your stated value, but should there be a claim and the research indicates that the values were overstated, you will not receive the degree of coverage contemplated in your coverage agreement. Just as with jewels, fine art, or furs, if you over-insure your property, all that you accomplish is making the insurance company wealthier.

An insurance appraisal should be calculated based upon the replace-ment cost—the price you would have to pay if you went out and replaced the collection buying from dealers or at auction. It should not matter whether you paid $10,000 for the collection or $200,000; if it would cost $100,000 to replace it today that is the exact amount that it should be insured for. The pertinent point is that this is a retail appraisal, probably the only appraisal that is most beneficial to the owner. You should be completely certain and satisfied that the appraiser understands that the purpose is for insurance, as most appraisals are for liquidation value. The appraisal report should clearly state that it uses Retail Replacement Value for the purpose of obtaining and maintaining insurance coverage.

Premiums may vary by company, but by far, the least expensive coverage is in force when your collection always remains inside a safe deposit box at a financial institution. This insurance may seem unnecessary, but in the 1980s, a substantial collection of a prominent coin collector was stolen from his safe-deposit box when a large bank in Boston was vandalized over the weekend. Another client's bank vault was flooded for five entire days. Instances like this are rare, but they do happen.

Generally insurance companies charge one-half percent of the value of the collection for annual safe-deposit box coverage ($500 for $100,000) and at least double that amount if you require coverage outside the bank. Special circumstances may require additional premiums, so read the policy language carefully for exceptions and ask any questions you believe are necessary for you to fully understand the policy.

The reputation of the insurance company is also very important. There are certain insurance companies that will strongly dispute each and every claim made by a client, and some are very slow to pay a claim, while other carriers are reasonable and will not dispute a valid claim. Ask other collectors for a recommendation and ask the insurance agent what experience the insurance firm has in covering your specific type of property.

Appraisal for Divorce

If you are in the process of seeking a divorce and a collection is among the marital assets, you will probably be required to obtain an appraisal.

Finances permitting, one party may want to keep the collection rather than have it sold and the proceeds divided between the parties. This could create one more conflict during the divorce. The spouse that would like to maintain the collection will solicit a low appraisal, while the opposing spouse, who wishes to sell, will look for a higher appraisal.

The most equitable resolution for a divorce appraisal is to show the collection to two or three reputable appraisers (three is optimal, but may be unnecessary and expensive if the first two are within 20% of each other). In a divorce, the value definition is set by the state and varies from jurisdiction to jurisdiction. Although many times the regulations ask for fair market value, double check with the court how the marital property must be valued. Expect the appraiser to have a completed appraisal available within a reasonable amount of time depending on the complexity of the appraisal.

The most common issue is where one party is interested in the residence or other assets and the other party has an interest in a work of art or a collectible. How should the assets be valued and the property divided among the parties?

Selecting an Appraiser

Selecting the appraiser is the most important part of this process. In addition to the qualifications mentioned earlier, you are searching for an expert who will represent your best interests in providing a knowledgeable and honest evaluation of your collection. Further, the evaluation should match the needs of the situation being addressed. But you still need to retain the responsibility of protecting your own interests.

In general, appraisers should belong to one of the three appraisal organizations mentioned earlier – AAA, ASA and ISA – as these organizations require continuing education of their members and ensure that members prepare reports in compliance with both USPAP and the standards of the appraisal organization.

If you have a coin collection, your appraiser should be a life member of the American Numismatic Association (ANA), a member of the Professional Numismatists Guild (PNG), have at least five years of experience as a professional numismatist, be able to provide financial references from a reliable bank and have a solid reputation among knowledgeable collectors. This is the ideal. Depending on your location and the relative value of your collection, you may choose to settle for less, but these are the qualifications you should be seeking. If you have a significant collection, it is probably in your best interests to incur higher expenses (if necessary) to engage an appraiser at this level. Remember, such expenses are usually deductible and the ramifications of a poorly executed appraisal may result in substantial issues down the line.

Appraisers may be located in private practice, galleries, auction houses, or many other professions. What is crucial is to select an appraiser who has expertise in the specialty you need. The appraiser should have up-to-date knowledge of the current market place, appraisal practice experience, and knowledge and compliance with USPAP and ethical standards. USPAP is revised every two years and appraisal organizations require members to take an update course every two years. Ask your appraiser when the last time he or she took the 7-hour USPAP update class.

For highly valued estates or large charitable donations, where IRS scrutiny is to be anticipated, selecting the appropriate "qualified appraiser" will be of importance in resolving or eliminating any disputes that may arise. Be certain to request a resume from the prospective appraisers and review it carefully to evaluate their background, relevant certifications, education and work experience.

What Will it Cost?

A formal appraisal can be an expensive undertaking. Expect to pay $175 an hour on average. An appraiser in a small town may charge $100-$175 per hour, while appraisers in larger cities or "high rent" districts tend to charge $200-$400 per hour. If the collection is significant, and the material is rare or esoteric—or if the situation is complex or unusually contentious—you may need the services of a top-rate professional. Their rates can top $500 per hour. We would emphasize, however, that such a level of expertise is necessary only for the most complex projects and objects.

In searching for an appraiser, be clear in communicating what you have and the kind of appraisal you need, then ask for an approximate

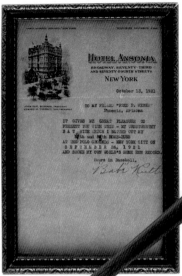

1921 Babe Ruth Personally Documented Home Run Bat Attributed to Record 59th of the Season, PSA/DNA GU 10.
Sold for: $717,000 | February 2015

fee after discussing the scope and purpose of the appraisal. If the appraiser won't commit to an exact cost and time estimate ("Two to three hours, no more than three," for example), find someone who will. It is generally unethical for an appraiser to charge a fee that is contingent on value, so if an appraiser offers to charge based on a percentage of assessed value, be cautious. Remember, a "one price," liquidation appraisal will require much less time (and expense) than a line by line, individually-bid "grocery list." As a general rule, less complex appraisals are less expensive since appraisers are paid hourly.

There may be no costs involved in certain circumstances. Some dealers will provide you with a dated, written offer to purchase your collectibles on a no-obligation basis. That offer will be acceptable as a liquidation appraisal. Others dealers may charge you for a written appraisal with the caveat that if you sell them the collection by a given date, the appraisal fees will be rebated. Dealers would much rather purchase collections than appraise them and you can use that leverage to your advantage. In all fairness, however, if someone does a "free" appraisal, you should at least allow them the opportunity to bid when you make a decision to sell.

You May Not Need an Appraisal Report

If you are not filing a tax return, donating non-cash assets to a non-profit, or obtaining insurance for your collectibles, you may not need a qualified appraisal report. The expense and time required to develop a formal appraisal may be avoided in certain circumstances. Many uninformed people mistakenly seek an appraisal when only general guidance as to value is required.

If your objective is to sell your collection, and you are interested in determining the amount a dealer would pay for your collection, most dealers will be pleased to make an offer or provide you with their best estimate of value without the labor and expense of creating a formal appraisal report. Similarly, an auction house will usually provide you with an auction estimate free of charge based upon the possibility of its being selected to auction the contents of your collection.

Independent appraisers can also evaluate property and provide a verbal appraisal of the property for less than a formal written appraisal because less of the appraiser's time is utilized.

Safety of Collectibles During Appraisal

It is your responsibility to ensure the safety of your collection during the appraisal. You should expect it to cost more, but once you have selected an appraiser, the safest method is to have the appraiser meet with you at a bank. A true professional will generate an inventory if one does not already exist and then make evaluation notes in the safe deposit room. The appraiser will then take the notes back to their office to determine values and draft the appraisal. Explain the time frame to the appraiser and don't forget to request an estimate for their time. Even a modest collection, appraised under these ideal conditions (ideal for you, but not necessarily for the dealer) will probably be charged at several hours.

A less expensive alternative is to transport the collectibles to the dealer and remain with them when the appraisal notes are being made. You can then return at an agreed-upon date to procure the appraisal. If your location or schedule requires you to either ship or leave your collection for appraisal, you should put more effort into qualifying your appraiser. This is simply good business and a natural step in assuring the safety of your collection. Most independent appraisers are highly reluctant to take possession of property and should you send property to an appraiser, you should have a clear understanding of who's insurance is covering the property when it's in the appraiser's care.

In summary, after you determine the scope of your collection and what you are attempting to accomplish with an appraisal you should select the professional who combines the qualifications and fee-structure best suited to your needs, and safeguard your collection during the process.

The Appraisal Report

To meet all the current professional standards, an appraisal report prepared for any purpose will need to contain certain information:

- The property owner's name and address;
- The name, contact information, tax payer ID and qualifications of the appraiser;
- The purpose of the appraisal;
- The valuation approach employed;
- The value definition used;
- A marketplace analysis;
- Date of inspection;
- Cost, date and manner of acquisition of the subject property, if known;
- Current opinion of value;
- Effective date of the appraisal;
- Date of document;
- A detailed catalog description of each item following the Getty;
- Object ID format;
- Supporting evidence (comparable past sales data);
- A host of other formal and content requirements, including, believe it or not, pagination style.

All of the requirements governing appraisals fall under two goals: ensuring that the appraiser is competent and ensuring that the appraiser is impartial. USPAP requires that an appraisal report of tangible property must include a Certification Statement from the appraiser which states:

- The statements of fact contained in this report are true and correct;

- The reported analyses, opinions and conclusions are limited only by the reported assumptions and limiting conditions and are my personal, impartial, and unbiased professional analyses, opinions and conclusions;

- I have no (or, specified) present or prospective interest in the property that is the subject of this report, and no (or, specified) personal interest with respect to the parties involved;

- I have no bias with respect to the property that is the subject of this report or to the parties involved in the assignment;

- My engagement in this assignment was not contingent upon developing or reporting predetermined results;

- My compensation for completing this assignment is not contingent upon the development or reporting of a predetermined value or direction in value that favors the cause of the client, the amount of the value opinion, the attainment of a stipulated result, or the occurrence of a subsequent event directly related to the intended use of this appraisal;

- My analyses, opinions and conclusions were developed, and this report has been prepared, in conformity of the Uniform Standards for Professional Appraisal Practice;

- I have (or, have not) made a personal inspection of the property that is the subject of this report. (If more than one person signs this Certification, the Certification must clearly specify which individuals did and which individuals did not make a personal inspection of the appraised property;

- No one provided significant personal property appraisal assistance to the person signing this certification. (If there are exceptions, the name of each individual providing significant personal property appraisal assistance must be stated here.)

- Subsequent guidance, Notice 2006-96, relating to the appraisal standard changes in the Pension Protection Act of 2006 also requires the appraiser to certify that the appraiser understands that a substantial or gross valuation misstatement resulting from an appraisal of the value of the property that the appraiser knows,

Birger Sandzén (American, 1871-1954)
Lake at Sunset, Colorado, 1921
Oil on canvas
80 x 60 inches
Sold for: $670,000 | May 2016

or reasonably should have known, would be used with a return or claim for refund, may subject the appraiser to civil penalty under Sec. 6695A.

Clearly, the days of the cursory "laundry list" appraisal are over. Historically unregulated, appraisers of tangible property are now mandated to meet higher USPAP and IRS standards. The USPAP regulations include a Competency Rule, which requires an appraiser to possess both the knowledge and experience necessary to perform any assignment undertaken, or to take the necessary steps to acquire this competency through study or association with other appraisers. There are also increased restrictions on who is considered to be a qualified appraiser for donation appraisals. The appraiser cannot be related to or associated with either the donor or the donee.

Appraisals of Collectibles – In General

IRS publication 561 includes specific guidelines regarding the appraisal of coins and other collectibles. The following is a summary of the appropriate standards recommended by the IRS for appraising coins and collectibles which are contained in IRS Publication 561, "Determining the Value of Donated Property".

This publication indicates that many of the factors that are significant in the appraisal of art objects apply also to collectibles and we will include those standards in our analysis of the factors involved in the appraisal of coins and other collectibles.

Though an appraiser is not an authenticator, an appraiser must perform due diligence in regards to authenticity If the authenticity of an object is not self-evident, an appraiser should consult a leading expert in the field when a question of authenticity arises and document the steps taken to establish authenticity.

One of the components in the appraisal process relates to the physical condition of the object and the extent of any restoration that has been performed on the item. These have a significant effect on the value and must be reported in an appraisal to the extent that it impacts the value.

It is important to select the appropriate appraiser. More weight will usually be afforded to an appraisal prepared by an individual specializing in the kind and price range of the art being appraised. Certain dealers are specialists in their respective fields. Their opinions on the authenticity and desirability of such objects are given more weight than the opinions of more generalist appraisers.

Publications available to help you determine the value of many kinds of collections include catalogs, dealers price lists and specialized hobby periodicals. When using one of these price guides, you must use the current edition at the date of contribution and note which edition or issue of a publication you used in the appraisal report. However these sources are not always reliable indicators of FMV and should be supported by other evidence. The price that an item may have sold for in an auction may have been the result of a rigged sale or a mere bidding duel. The appraiser must analyze the reference material, and recognize and make adjustments for misleading entries.

Publication 561 specifically refers to coin collections. Many catalogs and other reference materials show the writer's or publisher's opinion of the value of coins on or near the date of the publication. Like anything else, the value of a coin depends on demand, age and rarity. Another important factor is the coin's condition. For example, there is a great difference in the value of a coin that is in mint condition and a similar coin that is only in good conditioncondition and value guides provide different prices for different grades. For gold and silver coins where the value is largely based on the precious metal content, the spot price used at the date of the appraisal should be noted.

Some tips for book collectors: The value of books is usually determined by selecting comparable sales and adjusting the prices according to the differences between the comparable sales and the items being evaluated. This is extremely difficult to accomplish and should be performed by a specialized appraiser. Within the general category of literary property, there are dealers who specialize in certain areas, such as American, foreign imports, Bibles and scientific books.

A book that is very old, or very rare, is not necessarily valuable. There are many books that are very old, or rare, but that have little or no market value. The condition of a book may have a great influence on its value. Collectors are interested in items that are in fine, or at least good, condition. When a book has a missing page, loose binding, tears, stains, or is otherwise in poor condition, its value is greatly diminished.

Other factors used in the valuation of books are the kind of binding (leather, cloth, paper) page edges, and illustrations (drawings and photographs). Collectors usually want first editions of books. However, because of changes or additions, other editions are sometimes worth as much as, or more than, the first edition.

What about the stamp collectors? Valuations are primarily based on the standard catalogs available (Scott and others). Condition, supply and demand, liquidity, rarity and beauty apply to the valuation of stamps, as well as other collectibles. Generally, two prices are indicated for each stamp: the price postmarked and the price not post-marked. Stamp dealers generally know the value of their merchandise and are able to prepare satisfactory appraisals of valuable collections.

There are many collectors of manuscripts, autographs, diaries, and similar items. When these items are handwritten, or at least signed by famous people, they are often in great demand and are valuable. The writings of unknowns also may be of value if they are of unusual historical importance. Determining the value of such material is very difficult.

For example, there may be a great difference in value between two diaries that were kept by a famous person—one kept during childhood and the other during a later period in their life. The appraiser determines a value in these situations by applying knowledge and judgment.

Signatures, or sets of signatures that were removed from letters or other papers, usually have little or no value. Complete sets of the signatures of U.S. presidents, however, are in great demand.

Knowledge is power. Although you may not be the appraiser, this information will assist you in understanding the steps that are important to an appraisal and will allow you to ask the right questions of the appraiser.

The Beatles, Ed Sullivan, and Brian Epstein- Signatures from their
Historic First American Appearance on the Ed Sullivan Show,
February 9, 1964.
Sold for: $125,000 | April 2014

TIPS FOR HEIRS: If you have created a basic inventory where none existed previously, ask the appraiser candidly if the collection merits a full appraisal. They should be able to explain to you whether you are dealing with a collection that is of substantial value. That information should help you calculate the expenses related to the process.

At that stage of the process, we recommend that you expend additional time and energy to properly qualify an appraiser, especially if you are not a collector and are unfamiliar with the "players" in the marketplace. Be prepared before you start meeting with prospective appraisers. Often, individuals who request formal appraisals appear to create an adversarial relationship with the appraiser. This may be a result of an often mistaken belief that the owner knows the true value of the subject of the appraisal.

This strange dynamic often inhibits owners from disclosing relevant information to the appraiser. It might involve some previous damage to the property that has now been expertly repaired and is invisible to the naked eye. Or it may be related to the facts and circumstances related to the acquisition of the item. Regardless of their motivation, owners have an ethical and moral obligation to inform and disclose to their appraisers all relevant facts in order for the appraiser to make informed judgments that will withstand further scrutiny.

The obligation may be contractual if the appraisal agreement includes language requiring the owner to disclose any and all information known or documented regarding the subject property. Failure to provide this information, including any old invoices, auction records and past appraisal reports, may void the appraisal agreement and release the appraiser from any liability resulting from omissions or failure to fully disclose relevant information. An appraiser cannot accept any information provided to them as fact without independent confirmation.

When the appraiser arrives, show them your updated written inventory document, with all the supporting documentation and allow them to add value opinions to it. They will probably need to physically inspect all of the items and create their own appraisal document. Preparation will save you time and money. Heritage Auctions Appraisal Services (HA. com/appraise) can work with you on the proper form of the appraisal, the associated costs of producing the appraisal, and the timeline of completion of the final appraisal document.

Frank Frazetta At The Earth's Core
Paperback Cover Painting Original Art (1974).
Sold for: $1,075,000 | August 2016

Greg Rohan's Story

At the age of eight, Greg Rohan started collecting coins and by 1971, at the age of 10, he was buying and selling coins from a dealer's table at trade shows in his hometown of Seattle. Today, as a partner and as President of Heritage Auctions, his responsibilities include overseeing the firm's private client group and working with top collectors in every field in which Heritage Auctions is active.

Sometimes outstanding auction results are the product of a brilliant marketing strategy and the excitement generated by a once-in-a-lifetime opportunity to own something spectacular.

Sometimes. But just as often, pre-sale estimates are blown away by a confluence of coincidences — motives that have little to do with an item being exceptional, and end with a collector paying far more than an item would sell for on any other day. My favorite example of this phenomenon came on August 7th, 2000, when we sold a 1919 Denver mint dime from the collection of a New Jersey State Senator named Lou Bassano; Bassano was a devoted collector in his late fifties and, at the urging of his wife, he was selling off part of his coin collection to diversify his assets. The 1919 dime was in beautiful condition — the book value was around $30,000 but given its scarcity, we thought it could sell for perhaps $50,000.

By the time the auction started, Internet bidding had driven it up to $60,000, and Mr. Bassano and his wife were at the sale, looking quite pleased. Then the floor bidding started. It quickly climbed past $100,000, at which point there were two bidders left: a well-known collector sitting in the back with his wife, and a well-known dealer sitting in the front row, bidding on behalf of a collector with a discrete wave of his pen to preserve anonymity.

But I noticed something funny about the bidder in the back of the room: his wife was doing the bidding. Normally he did the bidding but this time he was arguing with his wife who was gleefully waving her paddle, keeping the auction going. I was puzzled; did his wife even collect coins? What was going on?

By the time the bidding ended, the dealer in the front row was the winner at $218,500. The room broke into applause and I walked over to the couple in the back to console them on their defeat and thank them for driving up the price. The man was relieved: "Thank God we didn't get that," he said. "She's crazy." His wife explained that it was his birthday, and that it was the last coin he needed to complete a set: so she'd bid as high as he would let her, ignoring his pleas that it wasn't worth that much.

The next day I went over to see the dealer to deliver his purchase and collect a check. "You were quite the star," I told him.

"I've got a huge problem," he said. "How on earth could that sell for $218,500?"

"Well clearly it did," I replied. He explained that he'd purchased it on behalf of a client who hadn't bothered giving him a limit. He'd been told to buy the coin that was expected to sell in the $30,000-$50,000 range, totally unaware that the bidding would carry it to more than four times the high estimate.

"He told me to just buy the coin," he said nervously. "But I can just hear him saying 'I told you to buy the coin, not take a leave of your senses.' I don't know what to do."

"Well the first thing you need to do is write me a check," I said. "I'll put it in my desk while you go talk to your client and if he gives you trouble and you need more time to pay, I can wait awhile to cash it."

Everything worked out fine in the end; the collector was of course shocked to hear that he'd paid that much for it, but he honored his commitment. I think that Senator Bassano probably got in more than a few "I told you so's" on the ride back to New Jersey with his wife, who had told him that she didn't think coins were a good investment.

A Fancy Light Pink Diamond Gold Ring by Chopard
featuring a flawless 5.07 carat heart-shaped diamond.
Sold for: $605,000 | May 2015

PART FOUR

Selling Your Collection

11

Selling Your Collection Through Outright Sale

This chapter is the first of three that outline specific methods for selling your collection. There are pros and cons to each method, but the general rule for selling anything is that "time is money."

This means that, all other things being equal, the sooner that you receive payment for your collection—and the less effort you put into the sale—the less money you are likely to receive. Our goal is help you make a measured decision about the amount of time you are willing to invest in the disposition process.

Outright sale is without question the easiest method of selling a whole or partial collection. You present the articles to one or more buyers. They make offers. You either accept or decline. The time you are investing in this process is limited to the period you are present with the collectibles at the evaluation(s); if you accept an offer, you receive your payment and go on with your life. If you assembled the collection, this can be devastating or it can be cathartic, but it won't take forever.

First, we will assume that you are offering a collection of substance to a dealer who specializes in the field. Specialized dealers are most likely to be able and willing buy an entire collection. It is also easier to locate them through their advertising and they can be qualified through their references and affiliations. What is the dealer thinking when you bring him your collection to bid?

Dealers are in business to buy collections coming through the front door (or through the mail). Most of their advertising and their longevity at a particular site are planned specifically to induce such an environment. Many collectibles are a fixed-supply commodity. If you're in the business, you have to acquire products to sell, and advantageous buying is at the core of such a business.

We have two parties together; one who wants to sell and one who wants to buy. Now comes the sticking point. In any transaction, the final result reflects the combination of knowledge and leverage of the parties. The dealer wants to buy the collection at the lowest price he or she can pay. Their leverage is that they have the money and willingness to acquire the entire collection and they also have the benefit of any degree of impatience that you possess, or that they can instill in you. You may also believe that they are more knowledgeable about current markets than you are, as a result of their experience and credentials. You, however, want to know that you are receiving the maximum reasonable price for your collectibles. Your leverage is that they do not want to let you out the door with the collection. Your knowledge and negotiating skills are also an advantage, as is any fear you can instill in the dealer about your willingness to not sell to him or her.

Another variable is location and how it affects the dealer's perception of competition. If you live in a small town with only one viable dealer and your collection does not lend itself to selling to an out-of-state or international buyer, the dealer's bid may be less competitive than you'd like.

A dealer is bidding on two different kinds of items:

- First, there are those items for which they know they have customers, or which are readily liquid in their retail or "high wholesale" operations. These are items on which they can afford to accept the lowest margins, because their carrying and marketing costs will be the lowest, and their risk of not finding a buyer will be minimal.

- Second, are the articles that do not fit those criteria: collectibles that are not routinely traded and which will require greater effort to sell. This particularly applies to bulky pieces, where additional shipping weight is also a factor. Such items will generally be figured cheaply because of the effort and expense necessary to resell them at a profit. They will take the time to find the "high buyer" because that is how they make a living, but their bid will reflect the effort and expense of finding a buyer and the risk of not finding a buyer.

It's easy to get upset with dealers for not reliably offering a price that is a good deal for everyone involved; ideally, you'd be able to count on the first dealer offering you what a collection is worth and that would be that. Unfortunately, it doesn't work that way—and your ability to achieve maximum value for your collection hinges on your knowledge of its value, your ability to articulate that knowledge to the dealer in a negotiation, and on your willingness to explore other options if you don't receive an offer you believe is fair.

Here are some tips for negotiating the best deal on your collection:

- Allow Yourself a National Marketplace
  The world has become a much smaller place through increasingly rapid communications and transportation as well as widespread Internet use. You should not limit your search for outlets to your hometown. If your collection is significant and of substantial value, potential sales outlets will come to you.

- Find a "Full Service" Dealer
  A large dealer with strong contacts will see your more common items as more liquid because they routinely sell this kind of material as well as the more rare collectibles. They already know who the buyers are and what they're paying.

- Create an "Aura of Competition"
  It is rarely a bad idea to obtain more than one bid on something you are selling and never a bad idea to let a potential buyer know that other people are bidding. This can be communicated after you get a bid: "Is this your best offer, Mr. Smith? I know dealers sometimes leave a little 'wiggle room,' but I have two other people bidding and this isn't that kind of negotiation." It can also be communicated before the negotiation even begins: "I want you to know in advance, Mr. Smith, that I'm offering the collection for bid to three people. Please give me your best offer the first time."

- Display Your Knowledge in Discussing the Bid
  Dealers and people handling collectibles respect those who speak the language. You don't necessarily have to have a deep knowledge if you can "sell" a few key points. If you have a few pieces in your collection that stand out, bring them up and try to drop in a little bit of jargon from the field—perhaps some arcane

reference that suggest a deeper knowledge of the field than you necessarily have.

- "Play the Player"
Follow up the responses to the questions above with further questions. "You bid ____? Isn't that a little low?" If the dealer can immediately address the questions with logic and explain his offer, he is likely at or near his maximum offer. Alternatively, if he's evasive or there's no logic to his response, there's very likely negotiating room left.

- Split the Deal
Rather than offer the whole collection in one lot, offer "test" groups for bid to get a feel for your potential buyers. Generally, there is more control when dealing with smaller, manageable "pieces" and you can often secure more money. There is also the "bait" technique of letting the bidders know that there is the potential for more to come. This perception may lead some bidders to treat you better in the early rounds. The trade-off is more of your time.

Fr. 151 $50 1869 Legal Tender PMG
About Uncirculated 55.
Sold for: $223,500 | April 2016

1963 Fender Stratocaster Sonic Blue Solid
Body Electric Guitar, Serial # 93726
Sold for: $65,625 | March 2016

Finding the Right Venue
for the Market

When deciding where to place an item for sale, a key thing to consider is how your object will be presented by the dealer, gallery or auction house. While a six-figure painting may seem expensive, each year international auction houses sell hundreds of seven-figure paintings as part of their Impressionist, Modern and Contemporary auctions in New York and London.

Heritage's May 2, 2016, Modern and Contemporary Art sale in New York was led by Abstract Expressionist Willem de Kooning's 1968 oil on paper laid on canvas East Hampton II. For Heritage, the important work was able to be a star in the sale instead of just being another lot among much higher value paintings.

When selling art and collectibles, do you want your work to be featured, or do you want your work to be a lot buried in a massive catalog? For East Hampton II, the painting was featured prominently in full page advertisement in The New York Times and featured in a national marketing campaign. It was placed alongside a museum-quality selection of American and European works by household names including Marc Chagall, Fernand Léger, Jeff Koons, Robert Rauschenberg and Milton Avery.

The de Kooning relates to his key 1950s paintings of women. As the catalog described in vivid language, "Here, a female figure emerges from an amalgam of sweeping brushstrokes in red, orange, yellow and blue. Subtle outlines distinguish her legs and body from her surroundings. The movement of the woman's body - her lifted legs and skirt -- hints at sexual pleasure."

Your exceptional objects – no matter what collectible category they fall within – should be sold in a venue that lets it shine and advertised to a pool of bidders who can compete for it. High quality photographs, accompanying lot descriptions and essays, exhibitions to possible bidders and advertising all helps introduce a work and its qualities to potential bidders.

The result? The painting Sold for: $802,000, at the top-end of its estimate of $600,000 to $800,000 and more than it sold for at its last offering at auction in 2011 when offered at Sotheby's Feb. 15, 2011, auction in London.

As Heritage noted after the auction, "This sale really solidifies our position as the leaders in the middle market, giving collectors and consignors the unique opportunity to see great works, often over looked, in an elevated evening and day sale settings."

It's tough to think of an $800,000 picture being considered in the middle market, but these types of works require a seller to ask tough questions of an auction house to help maximize value when it comes time to sell.

Willem de Kooning (1904-1997)
East Hampton II, 1968
Oil on paper laid on canvas
41-3/4 x 30 inches
Sold for: $802,000 | May 2016

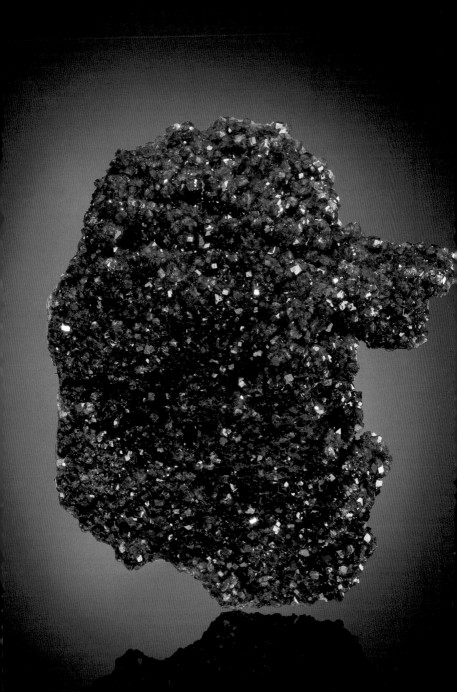

DIOPTASE
Sold for: $93,750 | May 2014

12

Selling Your Collectibles Through an Agent

"Sales are contingent upon the attitude of the salesman – not the attitude of the prospect." -W. Clement Stone

The objective in choosing this method is to receive more money than you would from a direct sale. The trade-off is that it will take more time and effort—especially if you enlist the services of several agents to sell different parts of your collection.

Many people employ an agent to assist them in selling real estate. The agent knows real estate values, has methods for attracting qualified customers, and understands how to negotiate. A good dealer has the same qualifications and contacts, but you rarely hear the term "agent" used in that context. Dealers would generally prefer to purchase collections outright, and then have the freedom to resell them without customer consultation. They may, however, accept a collection on consignment rather than lose the deal entirely.

It's often a good idea to offer a few pieces to the dealer to sell as agent to see how he does, rather than handing over an entire collection all at once. This allows the agent to focus more narrowly and allows you to maintain control. The key is regular communication and interaction between you and the agent. Items that the agent has been given may not sell and must be returned. The asking price may need to be adjusted downward. Above all, you must be able to trust the agent— to have faith in their ability and to be confident that they are looking after your best interests.

An agent is generally not worth the trouble unless they can get 10% to 25% more than you would receive in a direct sale.

The first step in seeking an agent is to determine the nature of what you plan to sell and try to match the right agent with the right product.

If your pieces are specialized, seek a specialist. If they are mainstream, look for the following kinds of qualifications:

- **Scope of Company**
  The agent (or their company) routinely handles articles of the same type, condition and values as those in your collection, and has strong customer demand for them.

- **Grading Service Experience**
  In the case of coins, the agent (or their company) regularly submits coins to the grading services and has a strong feeling for where the "standard lines" of the grades are. Ideally, the agent or other personnel in their company will have worked for a grading service and understand both the process and "looks" (eye appeal) that are most often rewarded on marginal decisions. The same principals apply for other collectibles, such as sports cards, stamps, and certain other categories. For objects like furniture, this may not apply.

- **Regular Show Attendance**
  The agent (or their company) attends shows on a regular basis where routine contact with other collectors and dealers provides a feel for the market and provides a wide range of business contacts.

- **Web Presence and Mailing List**
  The agent has an extensive mailing (and email) list and will present your collection to the maximum number of potential buyers. It's a perfectly reasonable question to ask a dealer; top dealers are proud of the size of their Rolodexes.

These qualifications promise the potential of significantly higher returns, but you also want to choose an agent who genuinely seeks the role. Many dealers only want to buy and sell collectibles, and really don't have the time or inclination to assist you as an agent. You should not be distressed if someone you approach turns you down; you don't want to enlist a reluctant ally. The last thing you need is a dealer who thinks they are doing you a favor by selling your collection.

Many variables can influence the arrangement you make with an agent, but these are the things that always need to be discussed:

- The agent's fees should be discussed and agreed upon in advance. Generally, they should receive a percentage of the selling price. This fee is usually graduated and predicated on the value of the collectibles. You cannot expect an agent to go to the trouble and expense of selling a $100 item for a 5% commission. A more equitable arrangement might be a 15% commission on pieces valued under $1,000 and 10% on articles valued over that amount. This is a matter of negotiation.

- A firm minimum price for each item or group of items to be sold should be agreed upon in advance with the understanding that the seller be advised before any articles are sold for less than this fixed price. Relinquishing your collection to an agent in exchange for a promise to do their best is not acceptable. It should be expected that the agent do some research and make a few phone calls prior to suggesting a minimum price. Agents should be prepared to substantiate the values they suggest. Similarly, you should not demand unreasonable minimums. No agent worth hiring is going to waste his or her time and energy trying to sell articles that are obviously overpriced.

- An agent must agree to be totally responsible for the collection while it is in their possession. The agent you select may be the most honorable person on earth, but he or she would still not be immune to theft or natural disaster. Proof of sufficient insurance coverage is mandatory. In many cases, the most prudent strategy would be to give the agent a limited number of your collectibles to sell at any one time.

- Negotiating the minimums is a critical component of this kind of arrangement. If you are not comfortable with the value range of your individual collectibles, it may be best to get a written offer first. Then you'll know what you're trying to improve upon before negotiating with an agent.

- The agent should be given the exclusive right to sell the collection for a specific period of time. Depending on the nature of the collection, the agent may have standard practices they wish to follow. Allowing the agent a set length of time to sell the collection should be separated from the payment schedule. Within reason, the owner should be paid as the items are sold. A good method to use is to make periodic settlements based on time or dollar amount. If the agent is given 90 days to sell the collection, it would seem fair to request that the agent makes payments at 30 and 60-day intervals, or when the amount collected reaches $5,000 or more. We would be wary of an agent who didn't agree to this proposal. Requesting periodic payments is also a simple and positive way to measure the agent's performance.

- Finally, make sure that you have the agreement in writing. Good contracts make good trading partners, and this is a business arrangement between two parties. All terms must be spelled out and the document signed by both parties in whatever manner creates a binding contract in your state.

One other area where agents can be useful is in moving "bulk" coins. Bulk is the bane of most coin dealers' existences. Some coin collectors have accumulated 10 proof and mint sets a year for 40 years and can't understand why the dealer is not enthused when three wheelbarrows full of coin sets roll through the door. The answers are: low price and low margin plus high (relative) weight. We can virtually guarantee you that if you have an abundance of this material in your collection, it will be bid very low as part of any outright purchase offer— probably 60% to 80% of wholesale price guides. From the dealer's perspec- tive, it is cumbersome, difficult to process, and likely to sit gathering dust while more lucrative products are prioritized. In some cases, like with certain U.S. Mint sets, you may be receiving less than face value for the coins.

Nonetheless, there are a few dealers who specialize in the sale of this kind of material and are the "high buyers." Your agent for this kind of material should know who those high buyers are and be willing to manage the administrative functions of arranging and completing the transactions. In return, they should either receive a mutually agreed fixed fee, perhaps 5% to 10%, and expenses. You should still come out ahead of the typical direct sale offer.

In summary: match the right agent with the right material, establish realistic minimums, put the agreement in writing and communicate regularly with the agent throughout the agreement period.

TIPS FOR HEIRS: If you are a non-collector and wish to use this option, we recommend that you obtain an outright purchase offer first. Use extra diligence in qualifying potential agents, and pay close attention to having the agent(s) validate the established minimum prices. Use the direct offers as a comparison and make sure that the minimums offer a significant increase. It may be even more important to offer small test groups to become more comfortable with the process and the agent.

1954 Mickey Mantle
Game Worn New York Yankees
Jersey, MEARS A9.
Sold for: $406,300 | February 2015

Mike Sadler's Story ....

Mike Sadler has been a consignment director with Heritage Auctions since 2003. He attended the United States Air Force Academy, flew jets for the military and is a longtime pilot with American Airlines. Before coming to Heritage Auctions, Mike's unlimited access to air travel enabled him to attend coin shows around the nation, and to build a world-class collection that was auctioned by Heritage Auctions in 2004. He is known for his tremendous knowledge of rare coins, making him a trusted colleague to many of today's most active collectors.

My journey to the greatest discovery of my career began on October 25th, 2010 with a phone call from George M. Monroe, a retired Colonel in the United States Air Force. The coins he was looking to sell had been in his family for a hundred years — in a box in a closet for a substantial share of that time — and came, he was told, from an ancestor named Frank Leach.

I was intrigued enough by the call to think it was worth a trip and so the next week I landed in D.C. When I walked into the meticulously kept condominium in the Washington D.C. suburbs, I had a strong suspicion something good was about to happen, but no particular reason to think I was about to stumble into one of the greatest rare coin discoveries in U.S. history.

The provenance — directly from Frank Leach — was a big part of the appeal; President Theodore Roosevelt tapped Leach to run the United States Mint in September of 1907 — a position he held until August of 1909. Leach died in 1929 and 81 years later, his family was looking to sell a collection of five 1907 coins, re-designs in response to Teddy Roosevelt's disdain for American coins, which he had referred to in a 1904 letter (coincidentally, later sold by Heritage Auctions in 2012, on behalf of an entirely different consignor, for $94,000) as being possessed of "atrocious hideousness."

The rarest piece in the collection was the 1907 Rolled Edge Eagle with satin finish, in condition far superior to most of the other extant examples. I had a feeling that the 1907 Rolled Eagle was special. Not knowing anything about the transfer of rare coins, the Monroe's wanted to move slowly and deliberately, making sure they realized as much value as possible for their collection. Fortunately, Colonel Monroe and I bonded over my experience as a fellow United States Air Force Academy-trained military pilot, and the family trusted me enough to let me leave with the coins. When I escorted the coins back to Dallas for grading — accompanied by an armed guard, as all Heritage Auctions employees are when transporting treasures of high value, my colleagues confirmed my feeling. Heritage Auctions Senior Cataloger Mark Borckardt called it "probably the most amazing 20th century gold piece I have ever seen in my whole life." Then he added, "This coin absolutely blows my mind."

Ryan Carroll and Jim Halperin were equally impressed (Jim said it almost had the appearance of a medal, and was unlike any of the dozens of others he'd seen). They insisted we show it to Numismatic Guaranty Corporation chairman Mark Salzberg, who happened to be in Dallas for a dealer grading event. Mark covered his eyes in disbelief when he looked at the coin. "Oh my goodness," he said. "You just don't see those like that."

One of America's smartest, most ethical coin dealers had previously offered the family $300,000 for the collection, thinking that he could make a 10 to 20% mark-up on the transaction. Heritage Auctions' argument for selling the coins at auction was simple: With specimens that were unusual and fresh to market, a public, widely advertised auction is the only method of establishing fair market value. With more com- mon items — or pieces that have been sold recently — there is a track record on which buyers and seller can base a price. But with something like these coins from 1907, it was anyone's guess and without an auction, Colonel Monroe might never know whether he'd gotten full value.

Heritage experts had initially believed that the coins would fetch close to $500,000 but, upon having the coins graded, realized there was the potential for very considerable upside on the Rolled Edge Eagle, which NGC finally certified as PR67.

The coins came up for sale on January 6th, 2011, Platinum Night® for our annual Florida United Numismatists auction, the largest such event of the year. Pre-sale interest had been strong, and I was able to talk the family members into making the trip to Tampa to experience the sale in person. When the hammer came down on the marquee lot — the 1907 Rolled Edge Eagle, PR67 — it brought $2,185,000, an auction record for a $10 piece, and also more than any $1, $2.50, or $5 gold coin had ever sold for at auction. It was also a price far, far higher than the coin ever could have sold for in any venue other than a highly-publicized auction through a reputable major auction house with a broad base of satisfied clients. The entire consignment realized $2,564,500, and the Monroes celebrated with a glass of champagne.

As Heritage Auctions Co-Chairman Jim Halperin puts it: "Even the greatest experts often lack the imagination to predict auction values when an item is truly special."

Apollo 11 Lunar Module Flown LM
G and N Dictionary Lunar Module
Landing Sequence Pages PGNS-43
through PGNS-48 Originally from the
Personal Collection of Mission Lunar
Module Pilot Buzz Aldrin, each Signed
and Certified on Both Sides, with
Extensive Signed LOA.
Sold for: $175,000 | May 2016

13

Selling Your Collection at Auction

"A fair price is the highest one a collector can
be induced to pay." – Robert Hughes

The auction has always been and will forever be the best way to show a product to as many potential customers as possible—and to ensure that you receive as much value for it as possible. When the product is rare, competing customers are important, and an auction is frequently the best venue. There are many benefits to this method of disposition, but the primary one is that in a good auction (a widely advertised one with many bidders), each item should realize at least its true worth.

An auction is a truly free market where each article stands on its own merits. Every item is examined carefully by those most interested in it. If you have a collectible that is rare enough that it trades infrequently, its current value would have to be described as uncertain. In an outright purchase of such an item, most dealers will factor that uncertainty into their price unless they absolutely know they have a buyer at a certain level. A well-advertised sale by an established auction house, on the other hand, will likely draw the attention of all the known buyers—and any others as well. The collector community is generally a small one, and most serious buyers are aware when objects of interest are offered for sale, particularly at auction. When that condition exists, competitive demand will dictate the strongest result and produce the truest value for a particular collectible.

Finally, if you have something esoteric—an item that is not traded routinely—a good auction may again bring the very best price. At the very least, a well-publicized auction through a reputable auction house will leave you with the peace of mind that your item was exposed to every buyer possible in a transparent way, even if it didn't lead to a price as high as you'd hoped. Choose an auctioneer with a strong track record for the particular genre—one who has the clientele (both mailing list and attendance) and auction locations to put the collection in front of the greatest number of potential buyers. When looking for an auctioneer, you should consider the following qualifications:

- **Financial Resources and Stability**

  An auction consignment is first and foremost a business deal. As with contracting an agent, an auctioneer must demonstrate sufficient financial resources to ensure they can both effectively conduct the sale and pay you at the stated settlement date. They must also accept liability and provide full insurance against the loss or damage of your collection.

- **Longevity in the Business**

  An auction house is a complex operation that requires a great deal of development to assure everything flows smoothly: consignor and bidder bases, cataloging references and expertise, site setup and physical security, auction flow and administrative efficiency—and that only begins to touch on what goes into it. Go with a proven entity; it's your money that's involved.

- **Advertising Resources**

  Success breeds success. You can't have the top sales without great advertising, and vice versa. Look for the companies who are doing the major advertising in the trade papers and on the Internet.

- **Location**

  A company that is limited to holding auctions in locations out of the mainstream does not have the ability to attract a large bidder base. Some companies hold auctions in major financial centers with good regional access, while others rely on the Internet. Comparing web traffic rankings of different auctioneers can also provide an indicator of web presence.

- **Competitive Rates**

  Auction companies charge both buyer's and seller's fees to absorb the expenses of the sale and turn a profit. A seller's fee of 15 to 20% has become the standard and you should not have to pay more, unless your collection has extraordinary "bulk" or requires special attention. Indeed, if you have a significant collection, you may be able to negotiate a better rate.

- **Strong Writing and Imaging**

  Catalog descriptions and photography create the necessary excitement and demand for an auction's collectibles and provide all that is available to entice bidders who cannot attend the sale in person. Our company, Heritage Auctions, is a pioneer in the use of DVDs and online videos and extensive descriptions presented through the Internet as alternative cataloging media. It's clear that this is the wave of the future. Browse through the listings on an auctioneer's website and look at the photos and catalog descriptions for lots that are in the same price range as what you're looking to sell. If you were the seller of those pieces, would you be happy with the merchandising efforts?

- **Professional Personnel**

  It takes quality personnel—and many of them—to conduct a great auction. In qualifying auctioneers, be certain to inquire as to the number of people that will be involved in managing your consignment and what their roles are. Our company provides potential consignors with a video that details the auction process from start to finish, and other companies should at least have literature that covers the same ground. Any company is only as good as its people. Contact a number of reputable auction houses to get an impression as to how they will treat your collection. Also, read through the listings of employees on different auctioneers' websites. Do they have specialists with impressive resumes in the category you're looking to sell in?

Auction is often the best venue for high-quality collectibles, particularly if the items trade infrequently. A good auction attracts the right mix of bidders to establish the real value for each individual piece.

If this seems the best route for you, interview potential auctioneers to determine which of them combines the best business resources, venues and personnel assets. Some things to consider:

- Ask the auctioneer's consignment coordinator to evaluate your collection and make recommendations on which articles should be auctioned and which would be better sold by another method. Ask them to explain why.

- Do you wish to be recognized for your collecting achievements? Some consignors prefer anonymity, but if you wish the recognition, becoming a signature consignor involves two factors:

  - Your overall collection must be of significant value. This could vary from auction to auction, but for a rough figure, let's use $250,000.

  - Alternatively, you may have an interesting collection of a more specific focus—possibly all items are in one group or category. Don't hesitate to ask, particularly if there's a good story behind the collection!

- From an auctioneer's perspective, a few high-value items are preferable to a large collection of lower-value pieces, even if the total value is the same: the workload is lower. You might be able to negotiate a lower seller's fee if you have the "right" kind of material.

- Large lots are at the other end of the spectrum. Large lots are bulky, cumbersome to carry to auction sites and difficult to ship once sold. They are time-consuming to catalog and require a lot of extra effort to earn the same percentage as a single piece of comparable lot value. Auction company personnel are not very fond of the large lots in major auctions and neither are most bidders, because their focus is on the more "high-powered" lots. Auctioneers will take your large lots for a big sale, but you have absolutely no leverage, and that's not what auctions are all about. In most cases, you would be better off asking the auctioneer to bid the large lots straight up. You will probably realize greater net proceeds and will be paid immediately.

- Keep in mind that the lowest commission rate is not necessarily the best deal. The first consideration should be the auctioneer's ability to provide your collection with maximum exposure and promotion. Saving an extra percentage point or two is meaningless if another auctioneer could secure an extra 20% for your collection. Negotiate the best possible commission you can once you've found the best auction house for your collectibles; don't pick an auction house based solely on the commission.

- Some people sell their collectibles unrestricted and others place a "reserve" bid to protect them from receiving what they perceive to be too little. Our rule of thumb: Place reserve bids only if you are very familiar with current markets and have good reason to believe that you will easily realize more than the reserve elsewhere if you "buy-back" the lot. In most cases though, if you've carefully selected an auction house that will provide your pieces with maximum exposure, a reserve will leave you with the task of finding another method of sale with no particular reason to think you'll realize a higher price. Then there are the reserve fees—a percentage that you will pay to cover expenses if the item is not sold because of your reserve. Generally, the percentage is based on the overall terms of your consignment and how realistic the auctioneer thinks your reserves are. You should expect the reserve fee to be 5% to 10%. If the amount is more than that, ask for an explanation. Good auction houses are likely to be knowledgeable about what an item can reasonably be expected to bring and if they tell you your proposed reserve is too high, pay attention.

- Ask the consignment coordinator for the cost of photography and lotting in the auctions that you are considering. For example, in some auctions, the minimum value for a catalog photograph may be $1,500 and in others, $2,500. The latter auction, while possibly a better venue overall, might not be as beneficial for your pieces valued from $1,500 - $2,400. Similarly, each auction will have a minimum lot value. In some cases, it's $250, sometimes it's $500, and in the very best of sales, it may be $1,000. Most auction companies will allow you to combine items to reach the minimum, but there is a limit to the number that may be used and still receive individual, mainstream placement. The key point for you to remember is that if your overall consignment is a good one, you may be able to negotiate a more lenient lot and photography standard.

Internet Auctions

Online auction websites like eBay allow you to sell your items at auction yourself, with exposure to a wide variety of bidders at a commission far lower than what you'd pay trough a traditional auction house. The question is whether this is a good idea. Consider the following questions:

Marketing at Work   The Harry Potter Chair

When a unique item with broad popular appeal comes to auction, anything can happen. Such was the case with the chair that J.K. Rowling sat upon while writing the first two books in the Harry Potter series. It was painted and signed by Rowling herself.

As CNN observed, "At first glance, it looks like a shabby, wooden chair with colorful graffiti scrawled on it." But those scribbles say, "You may not / find me pretty / but don't judge / on what you see," and "I wrote / Harry Potter / while sitting / on this chair." "Gryffindor" is painted on the cross stretcher under the seat.

The catalog description described the chair's history in vivid detail: "During her days as an impoverished single mother in Edinburgh, J.K. Rowling was given a free set of four chairs for her council flat-a social housing unit provided by the British government. This set included a standard 1930's era oak chair with a replacement burlap seat decorated with a red thistle. The latter being one of the more comfortable chairs amongst the bunch, she favored it to sit in whilst writing the first drafts of Harry Potter and the Philosopher's Stone and Harry Potter and the Chamber of Secrets - the first two books of a seven part series that would become an international phenomenon."

The chair would be donated to a small auction in 2002 called Chair-ish a Child in aid of the National Society for the Prevention of Cruelty to Children (NSPCC) where it Sold for: $21,000. For this auction, Rowling used gold, rose, and green paints to transform the chair into a magical piece of literary memorabilia, fearing that the chair in its original form would look like it had been "purchased from a junk shop for a tenner."

When it traded next in 2009 in an eBay auction benefiting the charitable organization Books Abroad, it sold for the U.S. equivalent of nearly $30,000. It was purchased by Gerald Gray, the CEO of AutoKontrol USA, who consigned it with Heritage in 2016. Gray planned to donate 10 percent of the winning price to Lumos, Rowling's children's charity.

Heritage shared the story with media outlets around the world, a physical object representative of a woman's against-all-odds struggle to share her creative vision. In a letter accompanying the chair, Rowling said, "My nostalgic side is quite sad to see it go, but my back isn't."

As part of Heritage Auction's global public relations campaign, the chair went on display at its Park Avenue, New York, office on a custom rotating platform. For weeks, families posed for photos with what is arguably the most important piece of Harry Potter memorabilia that exists. The $394,000 it brought at Heritage on April 6, 2016, was many multiples of its opening bid of $45,000. The winning bidder, who elected to remain anonymous, also received Rowling's signed letter "by Owl Post" describing the history and provenance.

Gray, who attended the auction at the Waldorf Astoria hotel in New York City hoped that it would eventually go on display where fans could appreciate it. But even if it stays in a private collection, through extensive marketing, Heritage was able to share the story of this magical chair with millions of Harry Potter fans.

Chair Used by J.K. Rowling whilst Writing the First Two Harry Potter Books, Later Hand-Painted and Signed by Rowling Herself.
Sold for: $394,000 | April 2016

- Do you already have a "feedback" rating that will give you credibility with the bidder base? Many Internet auction bidders are concerned about online deal-making with people they don't know. The equalizer is the feedback system that lets buyers and sellers build online reputations. If you don't have a feedback rating, many bidders will avoid your auctions altogether and others will bid less.

- Do you have the equipment and skill to create digital images of the articles to be auctioned? Items without high-quality images just don't sell as well. For quality coin photography, you'll need a digital camera and the knowledge to upload those photos.

- Do you have the skills to write descriptions for each item? Do you know enough about the piece—and how to grade condition—to describe it? Auction bidders are best motivated when a "story" is available to make the collectible more interesting. The visual image and description provide the combination that maximizes an Internet auction's results.

- Do you have the business skills to analyze potential problem situations? Can you collect a bad check or determine whether a "special request" from a customer is legitimate or a scam? Most of the people on the Internet are honest, but there are exceptions. Unfortunately, it doesn't take many bad deals to turn a profitable situation into a loss.

- Do you have the knowledge and resources to ship high-dollar packages to 100 different people? It takes a thorough knowledge of postal regulations and requirements, a considerable amount of shipping materials and insurance, and a great deal of organization and time.

- Do you really want to sell collectibles that might have upside potential in an Internet-only venue? More to the point, are you able to ascertain which pieces might have that upside potential?

We routinely advise would-be consignors to list certain items on eBay: Hummel figurines, common post-1970 baseball cards, and small quantities of items that aren't rare enough to justify a consignment to a full-service auction house. But for high-value items that require specialized marketing or a seller with credibility in the field, we aren't shy about saying it: Auctions are the way to go.

TIPS FOR HEIRS: A major auction can be the best option for heirs faced with the disposition of a valuable collection, particularly if you have little or no knowledge of collectibles and are concerned about receiving fair value. In this scenario, the auctioneer is working on percentage, and your best interests and theirs are the same: the more money you make, the more money they make. Additionally, the values will be established by third parties in the competitive bidding process. The real benefit of engaging a major auction house is its versatility.

Summing up all of the methods of disposition, certain collectibles are better suited for one method, while others would benefit more from a different venue. A major company should be willing to recommend the best venue for each of your pieces and divide the collection to your best advantage. Just be sure to ask. Heritage's Trusts & Estates Department assists in just such situations and can coordinate the sale of an estate through various venues and categories of property – HA.com/Estates.

Patek Philippe Very Fine &
Important Platinum Ref. 3970EP
Chronograph With Register,
Perpetual Calendar, Moon
Phases, 24 Hour Indication,
Diamond Dial, circa 2002
Sold for: $108,000 | May 2015

14

Etiquette & Tips

"Tact is one of the first mental virtues, the absence
of it is fatal to the best talent." – William Gilmore Simms

"Etiquette means behaving yourself a little better
than is absolutely essential." – Will Cuppy

The purpose of this book is to help you plan for the future and, if you wish, to help you dispose of your collection without being taken advantage of by the government, dealers or other collectors.

It is reasonable to assume that you want to receive as much money for your collection as possible. Similarly, it is reasonable to believe that potential buyers would want to pay the least amount they can. The one thing that's absolutely certain is that everyone else will maximize their own interests. You should, too.

There are certain rules of etiquette within any collectibles community. The first premise is the division of roles. If you present yourself as a dealer, you are automatically responsible for all your actions and decisions in the arena of that collectible. That means if you make a mistake, you live with it. It also imparts a certain level of responsibility toward those who are not dealers. Dealers trade with each other at wholesale levels, in part because they communicate in the same form of verbal shorthand that assumes a level of expertise. A collectible is presented, offered, inspected and purchased (or not) without fanfare, and the principals move on to the next deal.

Conversely, many collectors ask a lot of questions (and rightly so), are nervous about their acquisitions, and return a portion of those purchases after the sale. In return for this extra "maintenance," dealers charge collectors more and pay them less than they would another dealer. It is the way of the business, and perfectly justifiable, as there have to be both retail and wholesale levels for any market to function.

Naturally, most collectors would like to purchase at wholesale, and occasionally, they are awarded that opportunity. Usually, the key to this is demonstrating a familiarity with wholesale market levels, negotiating pleasantly and well, and asking only pertinent questions.

The same is true on the selling side. If you give others the impression that you know what you are doing, you will receive the best bid or options the first time around. We recommend, however, that you do not present yourself as a dealer. Some collectors claim to be "vest pocket" dealers in hopes of receiving higher offers. Usually, this backfires, as the dealer then feels relieved of any obligation he may have to point out to you unrecognized rarities. Be upfront, but be competent.

As a non-professional, you should be able to expect:

• An appointment to allow sufficient time to evaluate your collection.

• Financial and industry references at your request (and you should request them).

• Professional treatment of you and your collection, and quality security.

• You should request (prior) that any items bid at $1,000 or more be identified singly and that any article that would benefit from certification be listed.

• A written offer presented in a timely manner. The offer should be dated and any deadline noted.

• If the company has an auction house as well, and you request it, recommendations on which collectibles are better suited for auction or direct sale should also be listed.

• Prompt payment in good funds if the offer is accepted. If the collection is sold at auction, payment in good funds on the settlement date as promised.

The dealer has a right to expect certain conduct from you as well:

• That you keep any scheduled appointment and are prompt. This applies to the dealer and their staff as well.

• The collection should be as organized as possible to minimize the time necessary to evaluate and bid on it. Even a basic inventory indicating the location of each item is helpful. If the collection lends itself to grouping, this should be done beforehand. If one group out of the collection contains most of the "value," it can be presented separately.

- You should not "shop" the dealer's offer to other dealers. It's okay to tell each bidder that other bids are being sought, but you should neither reveal what the other bids are, nor the details of who is bidding. Shopping an offer for a few more dollars is strictly "bush league," and it can definitely backfire. For example, if your first bidder did not make a strong bid and you reveal the number, the second bidder may play the competition instead of the real value and you will come up short. Similarly, if you reveal the identity of those you plan to see, the bidders could collude with one another to your disadvantage. Remember, the aura of unknown competition is the strongest leverage you have to inspire dealers to figure the deal closely and make their best bids.

- You should tell the dealer "yes" or "no" in a reasonable amount of time, and that applies even if you accept another bid. It would be considerate for you to let them know the winning bid. They can learn from the experience and not feel that their time was wasted. That can be to your advantage as well, because if you bring back more collectibles for them to bid, they should both appreciate your professionalism and bid higher the next time.

Above all, you should both expect and extend courtesy. Do not waste time with a dealer who is discourteous, nor waste time responding. Ask and answer questions, but beware of becoming agitated, even if you disagree with something you hear. Your mission is to obtain the greatest possible price for your collection. To accomplish this, it is usually best to reserve judgment until all of the information has been gathered. The very person you disagreed with may be the highest overall bidder.

One final option for selling: Occasionally people ask us why they shouldn't dispose of their collectibles to, or through, another collector. The premise is that the collector would pay more and the playing field would be more level. There is some general merit to those statements, but there are some caveats as well:

- A collector will pay more for some items, but will rarely pay more for all of them. Take care that you don't receive a little more for the best few pieces of your collection only to find that there are no buyers for the less favorable material.

- Being a collector in and of itself is no guarantee that the individual you contact is any more or less knowledgeable or ethical than a dealer. In general, dealers are better-informed on current market conditions, upgrade potential and the reputations of potential buyers. We know of at least one situation where a collector acquaintance sold a collection for heirs, only to take a bad check from the buyer. That individual was well known as a "bad egg" by the dealer community, but the collector/agent was totally unaware. It took more than a year and considerable expense for the heirs to collect a fraction of the amount owed.

- As an agent, the collector is less likely to have insurance coverage for your collection while in their care. If you use a collector, don't forget to verify this just as you would with a dealer.

- Most importantly, few collectors will truly be interested in acquiring everything you have—and if they are willing to buy in bulk from you, it will likely only be because they are interested in getting a great deal.

The bottom line is that you should qualify a collector in the same manner as you would a dealer. Although collectors may have good intentions, a major collection should be sold only with the assistance of a qualified professional. It is unwise to rely on a part-time hobbyist to dispose of a major financial asset; a better approach is to use an auction to let that collector bid against tens of thousands of similar hobbyists.

Heir Relations

The final issues of etiquette are the relationships between collectors and their heirs, and between the heirs themselves. The collector, as the owner, has all the rights and responsibilities for the collection in his lifetime, and can provide as much or as little guidance as he pleases. Any guidance is better than no guidance. Even if few of the heirs have any interest in the collectibles, a general understanding goes a long way towards familial harmony. The collector should identify and detail any specific bequests he wishes to make. "Dad split them up that way in the Will" is a lot more powerful than "I'm sure Dad wanted me to have this one."

Similarly, the collector should indicate who should be contacted to help dispose of the collection—and who should not. It's amazing how many "old friends" can appear after the death of a known collector. The executor or trustee, whether he or she is a family member or not, should be advised of all these details.

Heirs should remember that the other heirs are also probably under a great deal of stress—so try to give everyone the benefit of the doubt. We like to think that family is the most important thing, so here are some tips to avoid controversy if the collection needs to be sold or disposed of equitably when specific guidance was not provided by the deceased:

- Leave the division to a third party. If the collection is not to be sold, have the appraiser separate the inventory into the appropriate number of groups by value.

- If one or more heirs want specific pieces, have the appraiser value those individually and if the remainder of the collection is sold, use those amounts to adjust shares accordingly.

- If the collection is to be disposed of, but each heir wants "something" to remember the deceased by, determine the dollar value that you want to set aside and have each heir "buy" the collectibles they want at the appraised price.

- In all cases, remember to keep things in perspective. The collection once provided a great deal of pleasure to your loved one, and try to let its legacy reflect that.

The preparation of this handbook has been a labor of love, though by no means easy. There are two main reader groups that have been targeted by this treatise, neither of whom should be overjoyed by the implications of having to read through it. If you are a collector, the thought of estate planning may make you look closer at your own mortality. If you are an heir or possible heir of a collector, contemplating a loved one's mortality is probably no more enjoyable.

We would take more pleasure in relating a more upbeat subject, but we will be satisfied if this handbook has made it a little easier for you to address a very difficult task.

We offer, in closing, this final guidance regardless of your circumstance or role:

1. Determine your goal.

2. Know your options.

3. Analyze them and pick the best course of action for you.

4. Make a plan.

5. If you need assistance, choose it carefully.

6. Above all, remain flexible and don't be afraid to adjust your plan as you go along.

7. Form a team of the best advisors available and pay the price now rather than later.

Good luck!

Ernest Leonard Blumenschein (American, 1874-1960)
Taos Indian Chief
Oil on canvas laid on board
16 x 20 inches
Sold for: $389,000 | May 2015

Jim Halperin's Story ....

Jim Halperin is the co-founder and co-chairman of Heritage Auctions. He formed his first rare coin business at the age of sixteen, then dropped out of Harvard in December 1971 to pursue a career in numismatics. He's also the author of two bestselling futurist novels, and endows The James & Gayle Halperin Foundation, which supports health and education-related charities. You can view his personal collections at: www.jhalpe.com.

Even though I'd callously disappointed my dad by deciding not to graduate from his alma mater, he remained steadfastly supportive. By 1975, at age 22, I was ready to computerize my growing coin business in Framingham, Massachusetts, and my dad, who at the time was 49 years old and had sold his own successful manufacturing business a decade earlier, offered to come in part-time and help me. I jumped at the offer. Together we set up the first full-fledged computer system in the coin business, an IBM 360 mainframe. And when we were finished, he had an idea — a sort of parting gift soon before he and my mom would begin spending most of their time in Florida.

My dad's idea was to setup a rare coin fund; he'd recruit investors to buy shares in a limited partnership, and I'd use the money to buy coins, store them in a safe deposit box, wait a few years, and then sell them at auction. Using his many contacts — and cold-calling on, among others, Fidelity Investments founder Ned Johnson, who invested $30,000 on the spot — he quickly raised $375,000. We called it the New England Rare Coin Fund. Now all I had to do was buy the coins. Having worked in the business since I was 16, I spent about 18 months slowly acquiring high-grade American rarities because I knew that those were the coins that sold the fastest whenever we had them available. I bought only specimens that I would have loved to own but couldn't have otherwise afforded to keep in inventory.

The economy had been in a moderate recovery when I'd bought the coins, but when it was time to sell a few years later, the timing could not have been better. By 1980, the Iran hostage crisis was under way, inflation had soared to 13.5%, and bank failures were heading toward the highest levels seen since the Great Depression. Unemployment was over 7%. Investors — from hedge funds to retirees — were seeking scarce physical objects unencumbered by complex financing arrangements, with aesthetic and historical significance that no oil crisis could ever taint.

When the collection was sold at auction in April of 1980, our investors in attendance stared in disbelief. Those same coins generated more than $2.15 million and, after all commissions, expenses and fees, every investor who put in $15,000 got back over $69,000. This, at a time when they had been watching most or all of their other investments tank. The profits from our little coin fund rescued businesses, saved homes, and even helped a couple of our investors avoid filing bankruptcy.

I was now 27 years old, and the experience would help me develop my own philosophy about investments — and the importance of owning a portfolio that Nassim Nicholas Taleb, the internationally bestselling author/hedge fund manager/philosopher, has recently termed "antifragile." That is, a basket that encompasses a diversity of assets, including some that are debt-free and likely to gain in value just as the world around them is collapsing.

Of course, there are many ways to diversify assets — but including some treasures that provide their owners with joy and beauty is, for my money, one of the best.

Joseph Christian Leyendecker (American, 1874-1951)
Thanksgiving, 1628-1928: 300 Years (Pilgrim and Football Player),
The Saturday Evening Post cover, November 24, 1928
Oil on canvas
28-1/4 x 21 inches
Sold for $365,000 | May 2015

APPENDICES

APPENDIX A

ORGANIZATIONS FOR COLLECTORS

Autographs

Universal Autograph Collectors Club

UACC P.O. Box 1392
Mount Dora, FL 32756
uacc.org

Founded in 1965, this non-profit organization publishes a quarterly journal and offers information on authentication and recommended dealers, and a list of dealers it recommends consumers avoid.

Coins

American Numismatic Association (ANA)

818 North Cascade Avenue
Colorado Springs, CO 80903
719-632-2646
E-mail: ana@money.org
money.org

The American Numismatic Association is the country's largest collector organization for coins and related items. Formed in 1891, the ANA offers extensive ducational programs and a monthly magazine, *The Numismatist*. Its Colorado Springs headquarters features a first-rate museum and library that are available to members and non- members alike. The ANA offers renowned summer seminars on a number of numismatic subjects and holds two conventions annually. These shows offer 250 to 500 bourse tables and significant auctions. The annual convention auction (held in July or August) is frequently the highest-grossing auction sale of the year.

Professional Numismatists Guild (PNG)

28441 Rancho California Rd., Suite 106
Temecula, CA 92590
951-587-8300
E-mail: info@pngdealers.com
pngdealers.com

The Professional Numismatists Guild is the preeminent dealer group in the coin industry. Formed in 1955 with the motto, "Knowledge, Integrity, Responsibility," the PNG accepts members only after stringent background and financial investigations, and a vote of the entire membership. Members agree to uphold a strict code of ethics and to resolve any complaints against them through binding PNG arbitration. A list of PNG dealers is available from the organization.

American Numismatic Society (ANS)

75 Varick Street, 11th floor
New York, NY 10013
212 571 4470
E-mail: info@amnumsoc.org
amnumsoc.org

The American Numismatic Society was founded in 1858, and is dedicated to the serious study of numismatic items. To that end, it has an extensive research library and world-class collections, and provides members and visiting scholars with a broad selection of publications, topical meetings and symposia, fellowships and grants, honors and awards, and various educational projects.

Minerals

The Mineralogical Society of America

3635 Concorde Pkwy Suite 500
Chantilly, VA 20151-1110
703-652-9950
Email: business@minsocam.org;
minsocam.org

It's not Heritage's biggest or best-known category—but it's pretty cool: minerals and meteorites. Individual pieces in our past minerals sales have sold for more than half a million dollars. The Mineralogical Society of America, foundedin 1919, offers magazines, books, and educational programs for the general public.

Stamps

American Philatelic Society (APS)

100 Match Factory Place
Bellefonte, PA 16823
814-933-3803
E-mail: webmaster@stamps.org;
stamps.org

The American Philatelic Society was founded in 1886 and offers members a monthly magazine, an authentication service, educational opportunities, and much more. Through a partnership with Hugh Wood, Inc. and The Chubb Group of Insurance Companies, it also offers a service for insuring stamp collections.

APPENDIX B

INSURANCE COMPANIES OFFERING SPECIALIZED COVERAGE FOR COLLECTORS

COLLECTIBLE AND NUMISMATIC COVERAGE

Cleland & Associates
3419 Westminster Ave. #301G
Dallas, TX 75205
409-766-7101
Contact: Richard Cleland
coininsurance.com

North American Collectibles Association
3002 Hempland Rd. Suite B
Lancaster, PA 17601-1362
800-685-6746
Contact: Barbara Wingo
nacacollectors.com

Hugh Wood, Inc.
(American Agent for
Lloyds of London)
One Exchange Plaza
55 Broadway, 24th Floor
New York, NY 10006
212-509-3777
Contact: Jack Fisher
hughwood.com

SEARCH EACH OF THESE NATIONAL WEBSITES FOR AN AGENT OR BROKER NEAREST YOU

American International Group
(formerly Chartis)
Private Client Group
aigpcg.com

AXA Art Insurance
212-415-8400
axa-art.com

**Chubb Group
of Insurance Companies**
866-324-8222
chubb.com

**Huntington T. Block
Insurance Agency**
800-424-8830
huntingtontblock.com

Pure Insurance
888-813-7873
pureinsurance.com

Marsh Private Client Services
pcs.marsh.com

APPENDIX C

APPRAISERS' SOCIETIES, AGENCIES AND BROKERS

Heritage Auctions Appraisal Services, Inc.
3500 Maple Avenue, 17th Floor
Dallas, TX 75219
214-409-1631
HA.com/appraise

American Society of Appraisers
11107 Sunset Hills Rd,
Suite 310
Reston, VA 20190
703-478-2228
appraisers.org

Appraisers Association of America
212 West 35th Street, 11th Floor
New York, NY 10001
212-889-5404
appraisersassociation.org

International Society of Appraisers
225 West Wacker Drive, Suite 650,
Chicago, Illinois 60606
312-981-6778
isa@isa-appraisers.org

APPENDIX D

THIRD-PARTY GRADING SERVICES

BASEBALL CARDS

Sportscard Guaranty Corporation (SGC)
951 Yamato Rd, Suite 110
Boca Raton, FL 33431
800-SGC-9212
973-984-0018
sgccard.com/grading-fees

Professional Sports Authenticator (PSA)
P.O. Box 6180
Newport Beach, CA 92658
800-325-1121,
949-833-8824
Email: info@psacard.com
Beckett Grading Services (BGS)
beckett.com/grading

COINS

Numismatic Guaranty Corporation of America (NGC)
P.O. Box 4776
Sarasota, FL 34230
800-NGC-COIN
941-360-3990
ngccoin.com

ANACS
P.P.O. Box 6000
Englewood, CO 80155
800-888-1861
anacs.com

Professional Coin Grading Service (PCGS)
P.O. Box 9458
Newport Beach, CA 92658
800-447-8848
949-833-0600
pcgs.com

COINS NEEDING CLEANING OR CONSERVATION

Numismatic Conservation Services (NCS)
P.O. Box 4750
Sarasota, FL 34230
1-866-627-2646
1-941-360-3996
ncscoin.com

COMICS

Comics Guaranty Corporation (CGC)
P.O. Box 4738
Sarasota, FL 34230
1-877-NM-COMIC
1-941-360-3991
FAX: 941-360-2558
cgccomics.com

CURRENCY

Paper Money Grading (PMG)
P.O. Box 4755
Sarasota, FL 34230
877-PMG-5570
941 309 1001
PMGnotes.com

PCGS Currency
P.O. Box 10470
Peoria, IL 61612-0470
309-222-8200
pcgscurrency.com

APPENDIX E

SELECTED PUBLICATIONS FOR COLLECTORS

Artwork & Paper Collectibles

How to Care for Works of Art on Paper,
by Francis W. Dolloff and Roy L. Perkinson

Conservation Concerns: A Guide for Collectors and Curators, by Konstanze Bachmann, Dianne Pilgrim

Caring for Your Art, by Jill Snyder, Joseph Montague, Maria Reidelbach

Baseball Cards

The Official Price Guide to Baseball Cards, by James Beckett

Books & Manuscripts

Antiquarian Booksellers Association of American (ABAA.org) posts links to member-published books and articles on collecting Rare Books and

Manuscripts

How to Identify and Collect American First Editions, Arco Publishing, New York (1976) – (out of print; you'll probably have to find a rare copy)

We also recommend: ABEBooks.com as a source of books on the Internet

Coins

The New York Times Guide to Coin Collecting: Do's, Don'ts, Facts, Myths, and a Wealth of History, by Ed Reiter

How to Grade U.S. Coins, by James L. Halperin

A Guide Book of United States Coins, by R. S. Yeoman

The Standard Catalog of World Coins, by Chester Krause & Clifford Mishler

Comics

The Official Overstreet Comic Book Price Guide, by Robert M. Overstreet (available digitally at HeritageComics.com)

Furniture

The Bulfinch Anatomy of Antique Furniture: An Illustrated Guide to Identifying Period, Detail, and Design, by Tim Forrest, Paul Atterbury

American Antique Furniture: A Book for Amateurs,
Vol. 1., by Jr. Edgar G. Miller

Miller's Collecting Furniture: Facts at Your Fingertips, by Christopher Payne

Guns

The Gun Digest Book of Modern Gun Values: For Modern Arms Made from 1900 to Present (16th Ed.), by Phillip Peterson

Standard Catalog of Military Firearms: The Collector's Price and Reference Guide (6h Ed.), by Phillip Peterson

Antique Guns: The Collector's Guide, by John E. Traister

Jewelry

Signed Beauties of Costume Jewelry: Identification & Values, by Marcia Sparkles Brown

Vintage Jewelry: A Price and Identification Guide, 1920 to 1940s, by Leigh Leshner

Antique Trader Jewelry Price Guide, by Kyle Husfloen and Marion Cohen

Paintings & Sculpture

AskART.com

ArtNet.com

Toys

Official Hake's Price Guide to Character Toys, by Ted Hake

Cartoon Toys & Collectibles Identification and Value Guide, by David Longest

All Collectibles & Fine Arts

Maloney's Antiques & Collectibles Resource Directory, by David J. Maloney, Jr.

Warman's Antiques & Collectibles 2016 Price Guide, by Noah Fleischer

For additional resources in all collector categories, please visit our Resources list at HA.com, where we also invite you to take our Collector Survey to qualify for free auction catalogs and a drawing to win valuable prizes.

Romanee Conti 2001
Domaine de la Romanee Conti
Jeroboam (1)
Sold for: $45,750 | March 2014

About the Authors

James L. Halperin

Born in Boston in 1952, Jim formed a part-time rare stamp and coin business at age 16. The same year, he received early acceptance to Harvard College. But by his third semester, Jim was enjoying the coin business more than his studies, so he took a permanent leave of absence to pursue a full-time numismatic career. In 1975, Jim supervised the protocols for the first mainframe computer system in the numismatic business, which would help catapult his firm to the top of the industry within four years. In 1982, Jim's business merged with that of his friend and former archrival Steve Ivy to form Heritage. In 1984, Jim wrote a book later re-titled "How to Grade U.S. Coins", which outlined the grading standards upon which NGC and PCGS would later be based. Jim is also a well-known futurist, an active collector of rare comic books, comic art and early 20th-century American art (view parts of his collection www.jhalpe.com), venture capital investor, philanthropist (he endows a multimillion-dollar health education foundation), and part-time novelist. His first fiction book, "The Truth Machine", was published in 1996, became an international science fiction bestseller, was optioned as a feature film by Warner Brothers, and is now under development at Lions Gate. Jim's second novel, "The First Immortal", was published in early 1998 and optioned as a Hallmark Hall of Fame television miniseries. All of Jim's royalties are donated to health and education charities.

Gregory J. Rohan

At the age of eight, Greg Rohan started collecting coins and by 1971, at the age of 10, he was buying and selling coins from a dealer's table at trade shows in his hometown of Seattle. His business grew rapidly, and in 1987, he joined Heritage as Executive Vice-President. Today, as a partner and as President of Heritage, his responsibilities include overseeing the firm's private client group and working with top collectors in every field in which Heritage is active. Greg has been involved with many of the rarest items and most important collections handled by the firm, including the purchase and/or sale of the Ed Trompeter Collection (the world's largest numismatic purchase according to the Guinness Book of World Records). During his career, Greg has handled more than $1 billion of rare coins, collectibles and art. He has provided expert testimony for the United States Attorneys in San Francisco, Dallas, and Philadelphia, and for the Federal Trade Commission (FTC). He has worked with collectors, consignors, and their advisors regarding significant collections of books, manuscripts, comics, currency, jewelry, vintage movie posters, sports and entertainment memorabilia, decorative arts, and fine art, to name just a few. Greg is a past Chapter Chairman for North Texas of the Young Presidents' Organization (YPO), and is an active supporter of the arts. Greg co-authored "The Collectors Estate Handbook," winner of the NLG's Robert Friedberg Award for numismatic book of the year. He previously served two terms on the seven-person Advisory Board to the Federal Reserve Bank of Dallas.

Mark J. Prendergast

Mark Prendergast earned his degree in Art History from Vanderbilt University and began his career in the arts working with a national dealer in private sales of 20th Century American Art. Joining Christie's in 1998 and advancing during a ten-year tenure to the position of Vice President, he was instrumental in bringing to market many important and prominent works of art, collections and estates. Based in the Heritage Houston office, he serves as Director of Trusts & Estates, providing assistance nationally to fiduciary professionals in all aspects of appraising and liquidating their clients' tangible assets.

About the Editor

Meredith Meuwly earned her Bachelor's degree in Classical Studies and Art History

from Duke University in 2000, and a Master's degree in Modern Art, Connoisseurship, and the History of the Art Market from Christie's Education in New York in 2001. After five years in the Antiquities department at Christie's New York, Meredith joined Heritage Auctions as Senior Consignment Director in the Fine & Decorative Arts Department. She now serves as Director of Appraisal Services preparing formal appraisals for over 38 categories. In addition to her duties at Heritage, Meredith is an appraiser on *Antiques Roadshow*, specializing in Glass, Silver, and Decorative Arts.

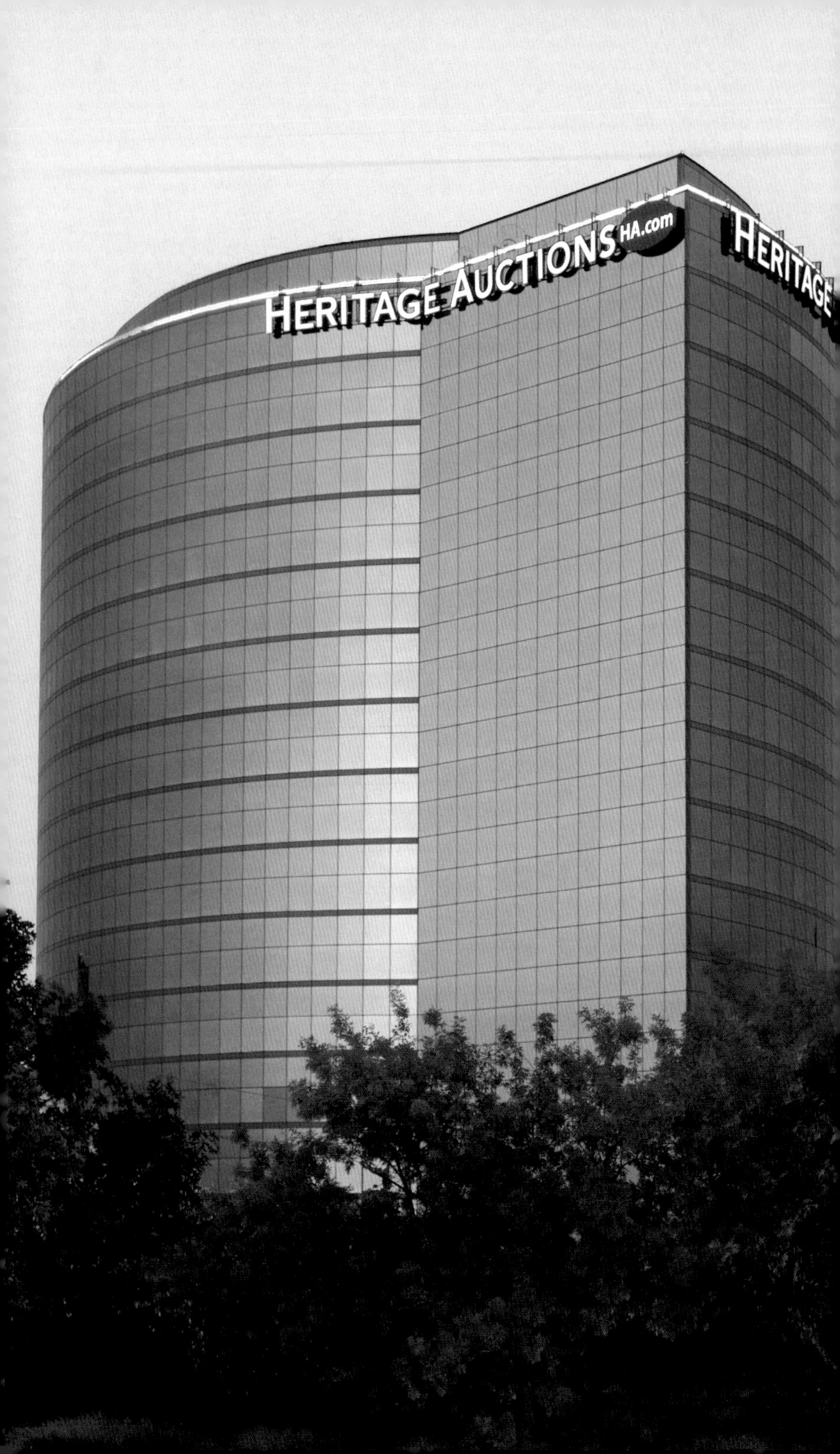
HERITAGE AUCTIONS
HA.com
HERITAGE

About Heritage Auctions

Founded in 1976, Heritage Auctions is America's auction house and the world's largest collectibles auctioneer with annual sales of approximately $800 million. Heritage clients enjoy unprecedented access to more than one million+ online bidder members and unparalleled standards of honesty and transparency as well as the latest advancements in technology via HA.com.

Through 40 categories – from U.S. and foreign coins to fine art and now luxury real estate auctions – Heritage Auctions offers a broad range of services for high net worth collectors, investors and fiduciaries from offices in Dallas, New York, Beverly Hills, San Francisco, Chicago, Palm Beach, Paris, Geneva. Amsterdam and Hong Kong.

Heritage Auctions offers consignors an unmatched depth of expertise with access to 3.4+ million prices realized and a network of 500+ specialist employees around the world.

We are always looking to acquire interesting items, whether through consignment or by outright purchase, and we spend or disburse millions of dollars every business day, on average, keeping our clients' demands satisfied. Find out why you should consign to a Heritage Auction.

Heritage Trusts & Estates Services

Individuals and collectors, as well as trustees, executors and fiduciaries responsible for estate tangible property, can avail themselves of the best suite of estate services anywhere, including authoritative estate appraisals, estate planning assistance, auction services and private treaty sales.

Inquiries: Mark Prendergast, Director of Trust & Estates, 214-409-1632 or 877-HERITAGE (437-4824) ext. 1632, MarkP@HA.com

Heritage Auctions Appraisal Services, Inc.

Heritage offers the highest caliber of experts to evaluate and appraise your art and collectibles. Working with our appraisal team, you will receive thorough, illustrated appraisal reports written in compliance with all IRS, USPAP and insurance standards. At competitive rates, a Heritage appraisal should be considered for all Estate Tax, Charitable Donation, Insurance, Estate or Financial Planning situations.

Inquiries: Meredith Meuwly, Director of Appraisal Services, 214-409-1631 or 877-HERITAGE (437-4824) ext. 1631, MeredithM@HA.com

U.S. Colt Model 1877 Bulldog Gatling Gun.
Sold for: $395,000 | December 2014

HERITAGE
A U C T I O N S
AMERICA'S AUCTION HOUSE

DALLAS | NEW YORK | BEVERLY HILLS | SAN FRANCISCO | CHICAGO | PALM BEACH

PARIS | GENEVA | AMSTERDAM | HONG KONG

Always Accepting Quality Consignments in 40 Categories

1 Million+ Online Bidder-Members